A.C. Burnell

The Law of Partition and Succession from the MS Sanskirt Text of Varadaraja's Vyavaharanirnaya

A.C. Burnell

The Law of Partition and Succession from the MS Sanskirt Text of Varadaraja's Vyavaharanirnaya

ISBN/EAN: 9783337817084

Printed in Europe, USA, Canada, Australia, Japan

Cover: Foto ©Suzi / pixelio.de

More available books at **www.hansebooks.com**

THE

LAW OF PARTITION AND SUCCESSION

FROM THE MS. SANSKRIT TEXT

OF

VARADARĀJA'S VYAVAHĀRANIRṆAYA

BY

A. C. BURNELL, C. S.

FELLOW OF THE MADRAS UNIVERSITY; M. R. A. S. OF LONDON;
MEMBRE DE LA SOCIÉTÉ ASIATIQUE; AG. CIVIL AND SESSION JUDGE
OF SOUTH CANARA (MANGALORE); ETC.

"Keine Mühe ist vergebens, die einem
andern Mühe ersparen kann."

MANGALORE
PUBLISHED BY C. STOLZ
BASEL MISSION BOOK DEPOSITORY
1872

Printed by Stolz & Reuther, Basel Mission Press, Mangalore.

PREFACE.

With this translation of Varadarāja's treatise on Partition and Succession, I continue a plan begun in 1868* of translating all the Sanskrit works on this the only branch of Brahmanical law now practically of importance.

All the treatises current in S. India however amount only to Five. Of these the Mitāxarā is well known by Colebrooke's admirable translation which can be improved only in a very few places, and as better MSS. now available show to be necessary. Of the Smṛticandrikā† my lamented friend Dr. Th. Goldstuecker left an edition and translation ready for the Press, but which was prepared nearly ten years ago. In 1868 I published an English version of the Mādhavīyadāyavibhāga, and about the same time made the following translation. I should have preferred to have finished first the Sarasvatīvilāsa (written about 1320 A. D.); but I have only got as yet two MSS., and these are insufficient to enable me to finish my translation also left nearly complete since 1870. This treatise is interesting rather from an historical than from a practical point of view. It will be valuable in tracing the differences of opinion which are found in the Law-books, as it contrasts the teaching of authors whose names only are now known, but it is, for this reason, impossible to consult it by mere extracts.

As there are already in print some 150 to 200 Volumes on this dry and uninteresting subject, I will at once say why I add to the number.

Hindu Law is almost a prejudged cause, in which sentence has been pronounced, without having previously heard the pleadings.‡ This is chiefly owing to the course taken by the man who most brought the subject into notice—Sir W. Jones. In an unfortunate moment this eminent man conceived the unhappy idea of being a Tribonian by deputy, and selected

---

*By my Dāyavibhāga, 8 vo. Madras 1868 (Higginbotham and Co.)

†This has been printed at Calcutta not long ago, but the text appears to differ from that of the oldest and best MSS. available in S. India.

‡Carnot, Notice sur Barère, p. 109. quoted in Grote's Plato, vol. i. p. v. (note).

as his deputy Jagannātha, a grammarian and not a lawyer.* The result was the voluminous treatise generally known as the Digest; Colebrooke's opinion about it is well known.† A few years later the true course was begun by the translations of the Dāyabhāga and Mitāxarā, but was not followed up to any extent. Meanwhile the English lawyers of the Supreme Courts who had to consider the subject practically, wearied of the endless contradictions they found at each page, set to work to find out the principles on which this law depended. Their materials were very defective, and as the doctrine of the Law of Nature was then popular and the historical school scarcely in existence, it is not a matter for surprise that the principles they elicited must now, for the most part, be recognized as fallacious. The most important of these is, that the Hindu Law of inheritance and succession depends upon the relations of the family This has been enlarged upon, and nearly all the Manuals in use are based upon this principle.‡ It is however entirely foreign to Hindu Law which repeatedly assigns as a reason for the course of succession that a çrāddha (or periodical rite supposed to be for the benefit of deceased persons) is more efficacious as performed by one relative than by another.§

A result of this erroneous principle is the creation of a presumption in Anglo-Sanskrit Law that a family is undivided till the contrary be proved. No doubt such a presumption is justifiable as regards a father and sons, or as regards brothers; but it is, I think, going too far to extend it to such cases as where cousins are living apart. At the present day Hindu Society is rapidly changing, and it is very difficult to decide by the criteria mentioned

* Benfey "Indien" in Ersch and Gruber, Encycl. 2nd div. xvii., p 238.

† "Two Treatises" p. ii. Strange II. 176. The Digest must however be of great value always, as it is likely to remain the only book accessible to the public from which a notion of the entirety of Hindu Law can be derived.

‡ See Mr. O'Grady's valuable Summary of Hindu Law as decided by the Courts, p. 2, where he writes—"*The Hindu law of inheritance hinges on the family relation.* The Hindu law of inheritance turns on the 'relative principle'."

§ The rites for the first ten days after death are supposed to cause the soul of the deceased to be re-embodied in another world; the çrāddha supplies food. So we find the materialist Cārvāka sect argue—"If the çrāddha gratifies deceased beings (in the other world), then it is useless to provide for travellers in this world provision for the way." That the Hindu law of inheritance turns upon this doctrine *alone*, was pointed out by Sir W. Jones!

in the Sanskrit text-books whether partition has occurred or not, as it mostly depends on rites very generally neglected now-a-days. Practically there can be no doubt that division takes place comparatively seldom though the Sanskrit Law expressly advocates it.* In short, the "family principle" has tended to confound questions of inheritance and division.

Another principle deduced by English lawyers is the doctrine of Schools of Hindu Law. This is unnecessary and foreign to the original texts and Digests. It is unnecessary because the real differences between even the Mitākṣarā and Dāyabhāga are very few in number, certainly not more than the constructions one often finds put upon some English Law, and it is quite beyond doubt that the authors of the texts and Digests had no notion of the kind. Nor does it represent any historical fact. Take the neat maps prefixed to most Manuals. One finds there the Madras Presidency divided into four states, according to the languages used. Now up to the Muhammedan invasion of 1310 and even a while after it the Tamil country was divided into two kingdoms the Cōḷa and Pāṇḍya. The Cōḷa kingdom is certainly very old,† and it extended once far into the Telugu country (to the Godāvarī). The Pāṇḍya kingdom comprised the South of the Tamil country.‡ Drāviḍa taken in the sense of Tamil is thus an inapplicable term for these kingdoms; as the Mitākṣarā is the foundation of Hindu Law in the Tamil country, no other name for the system of law prevailing there is necessary.

There never was a Karnāṭaka kingdom; I suppose that Vijayanagara is intended. What *Andhra* is supposed to mean, I cannot imagine. If it is taken in the sense of Telugu, it is quite certain that before most of the Digests were compiled, nearly all the Telugu country was under Muhammedan rule.§ Drāviḍa and similar words are (with such meanings) late introductions into Sanskrit, and belong to the latest sectarian literature of the Purāṇas, and to the worthless Māhātmyas or legends to prove the peculiar sanctity of temples and places of pilgrimage.|| "Dravidian" has

---

* Inf. pp. 3 & 4. Dāyavibhāga p. 8, § 7.

† It is mentioned in the Açoka inscriptions (3rd century B. C.).

‡ With rare exceptions, a Hindu king never styled himself as of a certain country or countries; he is always "Lord of the Earth", or "Universal Emperor."

§ V. Elliott's "Muhammedan Historians", iii., pp. 32, 86.

|| The words *Andhra*, Drāvida etc. are much used in the Skānda-Purāṇa, and the erroneous meanings assigned seem taken from that source. It is however notoriously a worthless composition, and in S India is commonly spoken of as the Purāṇa of rogues and cheats. Yet the Privy Council accepts such trash as evidence. Moore's Indian Appeals, viii. 372.

been used by Dr. Caldwell in a technical sense, but in the Sanskrit literature one would look in vain for a well defined use of any of these words.* It is also necessary to remark that it is impossible to suppose that any Hindu king at any time in S. India ever promulgated laws, as is done now-a-days for instance by the King of Travancore; the king always consulted the Brahmans who told him what to do. † They studied the matter deeply, and compiled manuals on every branch of law, but this was done to help their pupils, and especially to assist in controversy with others. They never published their works, for copies could only be had as a special favor; they were not sold.

The real authority is (as every one acquainted with Sanskrit philosophical literature must allow) that of the author himself. In India learners have always been taught to treat their master with almost idolatrous respect;‡ they may not question what he says, and an extraordinary value is placed on every saying he utters. To talk of Mādhavācārya's Parāçaramādhavīya as a work of "the Karṇāṭaka school" is (according to Hindu ideas) to degrade it, if therefore it is necessary for practical purposes to distinguish the differences of opinion between the ancient Pandits, it would be far better to use the names of the few existing treatises on law or of their authors, than to perpetuate an unmeaning fiction. Practically the matter is of little consequence, for there can be no doubt that too much importance has been attributed to slight differences between individual compilers, and that it is really only necessary to distinguish between the Dāyabhāga and the Mitāxarā. As all other distinctions are purely arbitrary, it is needless to say that they cannot contribute to a rational development of Hindu Law, but will only lead to contrary decisions by which the subject will be hopelessly involved in confusion.§ India is already a prey to caste and sectarian divisions of the narrowest kind; it is to be hoped that this great evil will not be fostered by mistaken notions regarding Hindu and local laws.

So much for erroneous inferences from the original works. Hindu Law has also been perverted by the introduction of European and especially English legal conceptions, and that to a very large extent. This mischievous practice was begun by the former Sadr Courts, and has extended even to

---

* On the use of *Andhradrāviḍa* = Tamil language (by Bhaṭṭa Kumārila about 700 A. D.) see a Paper by me in the "Indian Antiquary" No. x. p. 310.

† This is the rule at least, but cfr. Major's "India in the Fifteenth Century" p. 25 (of Abd-er-razzak's journey), where he states the Vizier administered justice at Vijayanagara.

‡ See the *Apastamba-dharma-sûtra* pp. 4, 6, etc. of Dr. Bühler's edition.

§ The "Schools of law" doctrine seems to have arisen in Madras.

the Privy Council. A few instances may be of interest, though, as the matter in dispute is finally settled for India by the decisions of that tribunal, they have no practical value.

Unquestionably the most important error thus introduced is the practice of considering Hindu (or Sanskrit) Law as universally applicable to all persons vulgarly called Hindus, or even to persons of mixed descent The notorious case of Abraham *v.* Abraham* however proved too much for the Privy Council, and the decision in that suit has been productive of unmixed benefit; but in an earlier case we have the strange construction that the illegitimate children of a married Brahman woman by an East Indian are Hindus.† The Sanskrit law-books practically mention only Brahmans, and exceptionally Çūdras, for the other castes do not exist; in S. India, they can only be the law of the so-called lower castes by custom, and it is very uncertain if there are any Çūdras at all, but in more than one case, the strictest Hindu Law has been applied for no good reason and without the least enquiry as to its applicability.‡

Again the doctrine of survivorship has been introduced in a case before the Privy Council§; a doctrine entirely foreign to Hindu Law, and alone sufficient to render the administration of this Law nearly impossible, for it confounds coparcenership with the state of division. The distinction between these two conditions is a vital one to Hindu Law, and practically it is impossible to overrate its importance. The only explanation of the misunderstanding which introduced this erroneous doctrine, is that indicated by Dr. Goldstuecker: "simply because their Lordships could not refer to the very law authorities conformably to which alone the case should have been decided, they relied on an irrelevant text of the Mitāxarā, and in applying the law of succession

---

* Moore's Indian Appeals, ix. pp. 195 ffg.

† Do. viii., pp. 400 ffg. (Myna Boyee *v.* Ootaram).

‡ V. Rāmalinga Pillai *v.* Sadāsiva Pillai, ix. Moore's I. A., pp. 511 ffg. and Katama Natchiar *v.* The Rajah of Shivaganga, do. pp. 517 ffg. These two Madras cases will suffice as examples; others occur in the earlier volumes of Moore's Indian Appeals and in Sutherland's "Judgments".

I pointed this out (for the first time, I believe) in 1868 in the preface to my translation of Mādhava's Dāyavibhāga. See also the remarks at the end of the judgment in Madras High Court Reports, Vol. VI. p. 341. Maine "Village communities" p. 52.

§ In Katama Natchiar *v.* The Rajah of Shivaganga ix Moore I. A., p. 610 ffg.

See especially the late Prof. Goldstuecker's pamphlet "On some deficiencies in the administration of Hindu Law" pp. 19 and ffg.

which is applicable only to a divided family to an undivided one, even mistake this text itself."

The doctrine that some (or rather in S. India, most) Zamindaries are not divisible as being of the nature of principalities* is a fiction foreign to Hindu and Muhammedan Law, and of English origin. Though it is perhaps not so objectionable as those just mentioned, it should be understood that it is not founded on any system of law current in India, but has grown up since the commencement of the British rule †

English technical terms of law have also been introduced to a surprising extent. In every case before the Privy Council, one finds terms borrowed from the English Law of real property and similar sources, between which and the Hindu Law it would be difficult to make out any satisfactory analogy. At first sight it may appear that in many cases the English Law-terms are appropriate, and supply a conspicuous want, if however the origin of the two systems be considered, it is impossible to avoid the conclusion that the introduction of such terms must eventually lead to endless confusion.‡

---

* By the decision in Latchmee Devamah *v.* Vengama Naidoo (ix. Moore's I. A. p. 86) a *Polliam* is also of the nature of a Rāj, whatever that may mean.

† Sir T. Munro (*v.* Gleig's Life, p. 322) appears to have been the first person of authority who suggested that the Zamindaries of S. India were not governed by Hindu Law. Actually as far as the Zamindars are concerned, there can be little doubt that but few have any pretence to belong to castes recognized by the D h a r m a ç ā s t r a, and many are certainly the recently Hinduized Chiefs of half savage hill tribes (cfr. Hislop's "Papers" ed. by Sir R. Temple, pp. iii., 5 and 12). Many however claim from the time of Muhammedan rule and still use Muhammedan titles (*e. g.* Mansabdar); that the Muhammedans however held the doctrine now current regarding Zamindaries, it is impossible to imagine. Bernier says of the Rājputs who hold land under the Muhammedans in N. India in this manner (i., p. 41): —"They might be said to form a species of pagan nobility, if the land were inalienable and descended to their children." Baillie ("Land Tax of India" p. xxxix.) has shown how the Zamindaries of N. India were formed; they were divisible except in a very few cases. See also "Selections from the Records of the Bombay Government" new series, xxxiii., which clearly shows that under the Mahrathas the sanction of the State was always necessary to succession to property held from the State, so Zamindaries could never have been recognized as partaking of the nature of principalities.

‡ So we find "heirs in remainder", "life-estate" and similar terms applied to persons having rights and to rights under Hindu Law. (Moore's I. A. viii., 544 and 550) The Calcutta High Court cases are full of such terms and reasonings from the analogy of English Law. See *e. g.* Norton's "Leading Cases," ii. p. 620 ffg.

The technical terms of Hindu Law are in Sanskrit very precise; the translations of them which are universally adopted at the present day are due to Sir W. Jones and to Colebrooke. The equivalents chosen by the latter are singularly apt, yet in many cases they have been misunderstood, *e.g.* a common misapprehension prevails in respect of the term "self-acquired" property. This term is used to distinguish between ancestral inherited property and property acquired by an individual, and such a distinction is necessary, because in the one case partition can be enforced by sons or coparceners and in the other it cannot. It has nothing to do with the claim of members of the family to share in such property, that depends upon another distinction which can only be made with regard to self-acquired property—whether it is divisible or not. In the Courts a common answer to a suit to recover property alienated by a former member of a Hindu family is the simple statement that the property in question is self-acquired; but such an answer is little better than none at all, for except in a very few and well defined cases, all self-acquired property is, beyond doubt, divisible. The principle that decides this question is very simple, and may be broadly stated—whatever an undivided member of family gains by use of family means directly or indirectly is *divisible;** all else (and this necessarily in only a very few cases) is his *indivisible* self-acquired property, and this last class also includes a few things which, from their nature, cannot be divided.† Thus all possible cases of indivisible self-acquired property are but very few at the most, and in regard to these it should be observed that the question as to whether such acquisitions are divisible or not, can only arise on partition. As long as a family is undivided, so long must it necessarily be impossible to predicate of any particular article, that it is the indivisible self-acquired property of any individual member. The general view which one finds prevailing in the Courts is the contrary and untenable.

This and similar errors have obviously arisen from an imperfect and fragmentary consideration of the original treatises, and reference to them by mere extracts. Hindu Law (if it is to be understood) must be studied as a whole.

* Mr. Grady (p. 70) writes—"*Self-acquired property* is what a person enjoys independently (!?) of any co-sharer, and is acquired by his own personal exertions without any assistance from the joint-estate, by gift" and so on. This is the definition of indivisible self-acquired property and does not include divisible property so acquired. So an important distinction is lost—the difference between ancestral and self-acquired property.

† Vīramitrodaya, f. 221, a. copying Mādhavīya Dāyavibhāga pp. 50 etc.

The above examples are, I think, sufficient for my purpose.* If errors which sap the foundations of Hindu Law have crept into the system as now administered by the Courts simply because the Judges and Lawyers have not had proper materials before them to enable them to decide, translations of the original authorities can never be superfluous. I do not intend for a moment to express an opinion that Hindu Law should be administered precisely as the original treatises would require; at present circumstances are so different and changeable that a development must necessarily take place. But except this be done on the foundations already gradually prepared by the people themselves, the new system built up at the cost of so much labour must not only prove a failure, but its ruin will be the ruin of Hindu society. The dharmaçāstra is an integral part of the Hindu social and religions system, and cannot be set aside or tampered with, but at the cost of a train of consequences little anticipated by those who would fain make changes and will not allow that the existing state of things is a necessary prelude to sound progress by natural evolution.

Whatever may be its future, at present the study of Hindu Law in India is in a deplorable condition,† it is neglected by the European and Hindu alike; and as far as my experience goes, a Pleader never thinks of referring to the original authorities, but is content with a perfunctory study of some worthless manual. Nor can a Judge expect the least assistance in details; the most important rites are neglected and customs alluded to in the dharmaçāstra are now hardly known by name. In the last ten years the Hindu Law Officers have been abolished, and the last two Pandits who held that post here are dead; it is not too much to say that one might now search through-

*Any one inclined to pursue the subject will, in Norton's "Leading Cases" and Grady's "Hindu Law" find ample materials of proof how far Hindu Law as administered by the Courts differs from that of the original treatises. Both authors are guided in their expositions by decisions of the Higher Courts of Law, and the interpretations there put on the original texts and Commentators; were decisions of the Lower Courts accessible to them, these differences would be seen to be in reality enormous.

†Mr. Nelson in his report on the examinations that candidates for subordinate Judicial Offices have to pass, has emphatically stated his opinion on this. Hindu Law is however studied to more purpose than Muhammedan Law; however little subordinate Judicial Officers may know of the first, they as a rule know nothing whatever of the last, and it is not unusual to find principles of Hindu Law applied *e. g.* the system in regard to partition. Report on Examinations for 1871, p. 65.

out this Presidency and not find a competent exponent of the Dharmaçâstra. Hindu Law will certainly never be studied by foreigners for its own sake, for it is uncritical and its history and growth are uncertain; it will never be considered a great fact in the history of civilisation, for it has always been the privilege of a few and the wrong of the many; but its study cannot safely be neglected in India at least, and certainly not in the present critical times.*

II.

It remains to say a few words about the following treatise from a practical and literary stand-point.

Varadarâja is an adherent of the doctrine taught in the Mitâxarâ, and only goes beyond it in one point—that he admits brothers' sons' sons as heirs after brothers' sons (p. 36). This is no doubt following the analogy of grandsons; and indicates a decided inclination to use this method of reasoning in his treatment of the subject, a tendency generally observable in the later writers on the dharmaçâstra, but which also is evident in the arguments of far older writers quoted in the Sarasvatîvilâsa. Varadarâja also discusses the charges for funeral rites (p. 28) in which respect he differs from other compilers, as he appears to think that any one who performs the funeral rites has at all events a partial claim. This is probably a result of the troubled times in which he lived. In other points his explanations often differ to a degree which renders them very useful in understanding the older works.

The original treatises present some peculiar difficulties of form, and as these have never, I believe, been noticed, I may as well briefly mention them.

The style of argument of the Pûrvamîmâmsâ (for that alone concerns the law-books we use in S. India) is most puzzling. I cannot do better than quote a description of it by one of the greatest masters of Sanskrit that has ever lived—Profr. Max Müller, especially as the treatise from which I take it has unfortunately long been out of print. He says (Ancient Sanskrit Literature, p. 73)—"This (appearance of confusion) is particularly the case in those works where the so-called Mîmâmsâ method of Pûrva-paksha (reasons contrâ), Uttara-paksha (reasons pro), and Siddhânta (con-

* Sanskrit Law might perhaps have effected for India what the Roman Law did for Europe, had the Brahmans its authors had the least idea of anything more than their own interests. What a contrast its history presents to that of the latter as it is told by *Ihering!* (Geist d. röm. Rechts, i. pp. 1—16).

clusion), is adopted. Here the concatenation of pros and cons is often so complicated, and the reasons on both sides defended by the same author with such seriousness, that we sometimes remain doubtful to which side the author himself leans, till we arrive at the end of the whole chapter. It is indeed one of the most curious kinds of literary composition that the human mind ever conceived; and though altogether worthless in an artistic point of view, it is wonderful that the Indians should have invented and mastered (74) this difficult form, so as to have made it the vehicle of expression for every kind of learning." As it is clearly intended to be used by persons who want arguments, it would be very rash to draw any conclusion from mere extracts, but the Courts in India seldom see any more than a few lines of a garbled and loosely translated (or rather mistranslated) text made for an interested person* and out of which it is generally difficult to make any sense at all. Be-

* I know of instances in which I am confident forged extracts have been presented to Courts of Justice. One patent imposture yet accepted by the Courts as evidence is the Aliyasantānada Kaṭṭu Kaṭṭaḷe a falsified account of the customs of S. Canara. Silly as many Indian books are, a more childish or foolish tract it would be impossible to discover; it is as about as much worthy of notice in a Law Court as "Jack the Giant-killer." That it is a recent forgery is certain for the following reasons: It professes to record events beginning with the year 1 of the Çālivāhana era i. e. A. D. 78-9, and it is evidently intended that it should be thought to have been compiled at that time, but the very first 5 lines show that when this was written, the Vijayanagara kingdom was the subject of romance and must have been long extinct, it is therefore later than the end of the 16th century (when the Vijayanagara kingdom fell) by a considerable time. The word Pāṇḍya seems to be a dim recollection of some of the Jain chiefs who ruled in parts of S. Canara in the 15th and 16th centuries, one of whom was called Pāṇḍyarāya. In the text we find pure Hindustānī words which can only have been introduced in the last century; e. g. Sāhukār, and Bārah (twelve) in the absurd etymology of the name Bārkūr. But the origin of the book in its present state is well known; it is satisfactorily traced to two notorious forgers and scoundrels about 30 years ago, and all copies have been made from the one they produced. I have enquired in vain for an old MS. and am informed on the best authority that not one exists. A number of recent MSS. are to be found, but they all differ essentially one from another. A more clumsy imposture it would be hard to find, but it has proved a mischievous one in S. Canara, and threatens to render a large amount of property quite valueless. The forgers knew the people they had to deal with, the Baṇṭs, and by inserting a curse that families which do not follow the Aliyasantāna shall become extinct, have effectually prevented an application for legislative interference, though the poor superstitious folk would willingly (it is said) have the custom abolished. However both this system and the closely allied Maṛumakkattāyam in Malabar are primitive customs, and it is of course absurd to assign an origin for them in historical times, as e. g. the Anācāranirṇaya ascribes the last to Çaṅkarācārya. Cfr. *Lubbock's* "Origin of Civilization" pp. 69, 100 and 101.

sides this there are other difficulties presented by the Digests, and it is necessary to draw attention to them These result from the technical terms with which Sanskrit books are always crammed, and which render books on one Çāstra perfectly unintelligible to those who have merely studied another.

The Dharmaçāstra depends for its method on the Pūrvamīmāmsā, and thus all the discussions which occur in treatises on it follow the method described in the extract given above. It again depends on and is closely connected with the method of the grammarians, and with their speculations, and from this source it derives the seemingly strange speculations as to the meaning of mātāpitarau (mother and father), pitarau (both parents) and also the etymologies which form a stage of specious development.* But apart from these, the Indian lawyers have taken from the grammarians and Sūtra writers what is really the fatal flaw in their systems. This is the use of gaṇas. The grammarians possibly to economise words, have adopted the strange plan of not giving all the instances of a rule, but simply the first one or two followed by a word signifying "etcetera." So whether the cases in which the rule takes effect be two or three, or several hundreds in number, the same form is adopted to express the class.

Now every Çāstra in which this system is used is supposed to have lists of such instances and paribhāshāh or keys to the technical terms, and these a teacher is supposed to know. In short, these are the premisses on which the whole system rests. At present this information can scarcely be said to exist even in regard to grammar, much less in respect to law. In the dharmaçāstra this system has made further development impossible It was begun by the compilers of Digests, and yet they managed to bring it in everywhere † I believe that in the original texts on which they found their treatises they only find a single gaṇa which is in Yājñ. ii., 143 (resp. 146), and is well known by the important part it plays in discussions on Strīdhana; it is ādhivedanikādyam.

---

* These grammatical subtilties go back to Pāṇini and the Mahābhāshya or about 2000 years ago. Grammatically the explanation may be correct enough, but other texts (e.g. Vṛddha-vishṇu in Mitāxarā ii., 1, 3 p. 207.) show that many old lawyers never thought of it, and there is thus good reason for thinking that the versifiers of the law-books used pitarau and mātāpitarau as handy words to eke out their verses rather than as the most concise way of expressing their meaning.

† There are many more gaṇas in the Mitāxarā than in the Dāyabhāga; in many other respects also the last work is very superior to the former.

The interpretation which usually finds favor—"ādhivedanika (gift on supersession) and any other acquisition"*—is certainly proper according to all Indian notions, but it may be considered as nearly certain that the author had no such deep intention in his mind in using ādya, but simply thought of saving his verse. If however we examine the Digests and Commentaries written later, when the earlier texts and their inconsistencies had been much discussed, we find these loosely constructed texts the subject of a most rigid interpretation,† and the system of gaṇas in full use. It is impossible that in treatises on Law such classes should be very numerous, nevertheless in the chapters of the Mitāxarā which treat of *inheritance* there are upwards of eighty. Some of these are plain and obvious enough; such are Aurasādi—the Aurasa etc., (and other 11 kinds of sons); Brāhmaṇādi—Brahmam etc. (i. e. and the other castes); Asurādi—Asura (marriage) etc.

The more important ones to a practical man however seem to beg the question, e.g. Kṛshyādi, adhyagnyādi, alaṅkārādi, açvaçivikādi, dānahomādi, patitādi, pṛthakkṛshyādi, pratigrahādi, vastrādi, çirobhūshaṇādi, çraddhādi, and samānodakādi. Whether the Pandits who taught the dharmaçāstrā ever possessed precise information as to what each of these terms included, is open to doubt; now at all events such information does not exist, and the only method of treating the subject is the historical method.

Other gaṇas (Çrīkarādi, Manvādi, etc.) show that differences of opinion were classified, and the names of writers holding the same opinion were thus expressed, but in this case more suitably. ‡

It may here be asked—Do not then the commentators and authors of the Digests as in possession of an authentic tradition give exact and authoritative explanations of the older texts? The answer must be negative. They have evidently received the original texts as something sacred, and they have applied the Mīmāmsā method of exegesis to interpret them, but with limited success. They sometimes cannot make out what the texts mean and give two

* Mit. ii. § 11. 1. C. "as also any other (separate acquisition)."

† e.g. in "patnī duhitaraç čaiva." Here ča (=and) is taken to mean that daughters' sons are included! It is a characteristic weakness of Indian commentators to make much of insignificant particles.

‡ Should the original texts ever again become a subject of study, one of the most useful aids would be a Sanskrit "Glossarium Juridicum." At present (as but few are edited) it would be impossible to compile a complete work.

or more guesses; in some cases they force texts into agreement, and in others have to correct or supplement them.* The use of gaṇas tends to hide deficiencies of this nature; it may be reasonably doubted if these classes can be defined with precision now, or ever were capable of it. The conclusion for practical purposes is that a knowledge of the principles of Sanskrit law is alone valuable, and that cases must be decided by these principles. Attention paid to subordinate details must yield unsatisfactory results and cause the greatest confusion.† It must never be forgotten that the treatises consulted by the Courts are not Codes or Institutes, they are attempts to elicit a body of doctrine from inconsistent text-books in many cases grievously misunderstood; they may help, but are not conclusive.

III.

Varadarāja is a name much used by Hindus in Southern India and well known to Sanskritists. The popular Laghukaumudī (a grammar) is by an author of this name. There are also commentaries on some of the Sūtras referring to the text of the gānas of the Sāmaveda and on the Maçakakalpa by a Varadarāja and numerous unimportant sectarian works are attributed to an author or authors of the same name not to speak of poetical compositions.‡ It is impossible to say whether these are all by the same or different writers, and about the author of the treatise now translated it is impossible to say more than that he was probably a native of the Tamil country, and lived at the end of the 16th or beginning of the 17th century.i.

His treatise has long been known. Mr. F. W. Ellis († 1819) proposed that it should form one of the digests from which he intended to have compiled a complete body of Hindu Law § as prevailing in S. India. It is quoted

---

* That this is the course taken by the *Commentators* and compilers of *Digests* makes it very unlikely that the original texts should have been preserved in their original state up to the present time.

† Even a legitimate method of discussion from principles, will occasionally lead to contradictory results; e. g. the Bombay and Madras views regarding Strīdhana. Mill (in his History of India) has justly remarked that the Hindu Law mistakes minuteness for accuracy.

‡ So the Vasantatilaka is by a Conjeveram Brahman of this name.

§ Transactions Madras Lit. Society vol. I. It is there stated (I do not know on what authority) that Varadarāja was a native of the Arcot province, and that he lived posterior to the Mahratta, and Muhammodan conquests, i. e. after the 17th or 18th century!

i. He was a disciple of Bhattoji Dikshita;

by the elder Strange,* and is one of the works from which about 1850 V. Parabrahmaçāstrin compiled his little Vyavahāradarpaṇa.† Its proper name is Vyavahāranirṇaya, but this now appears to be forgotten. and one finds in the MSS. only Varadarājīya-dharmaçāstra or Varadarājakṛta-dharmaçāstra. It does not appear that the book comprehends more than a treatise on Vyavahāra; at least I have never seen a MS. which contained more. Its chief merit is that it is brief and comparatively free from pedantic discussions, but it betrays the usual carelessness as regards quotations. Texts are attributed to wrong authors, and are often inaccurately given, and as there is nothing added to the stock texts we find in older works, greater part of the quotations may be taken as only second-hand. Indeed there are very evident traces to point out the Nibandhas from which the author has compiled. He once quotes a text as from the Smṛticandrikā (p. 3), and from this source he has evidently taken greater part of p. 2. The Mitāxarā is not mentioned by name, but passages, taken from it almost literally occur on pp. 54, 5. The whole discussion about the capability of women to inherit (pp. 39 follg.) is taken more or less from Mādhava's Vyavahāramādhava. These are also evidences of Varadarājā having trusted to this treatise on pp. 8 and 49. Jīmūtavāhana's Dāyabhāga appears to be quoted on p. 52, and some quotations on p. 39 are probably taken from Haradatta-miçra's Commentary on the Apastambasūtra, praçnas xxviii and xxix.

As regards the relative position assigned to the original texts, this treatise is remarkable as being based on the texts of Manu (Mānava-dharmaçāstra,);‡ it thus differs from all the other Digests used in Southern India.

The original texts quoted are shown below; in the text of the translation I have given everywhere (when possible) the chapter and verse of the original to facilitate reference.

Anonymous quotations—53.

asahāya (? Medhātithi)—38.

ācāryaviçvarūpa §—53.

---

* ii., 189, where it is mentioned by the Tanjore Durbar Pandits after the Smṛticandrika and Mādhavīya.

† Printed at Madras in 8 vo. Telugu character (1851).

‡ *Mr. F. W. Ellis* was in error where he stated that it is based on Nārada.

§ Quoted in the Dāyabhāga and most digests. One writer of this name appears to have commented on Yājñavalkya.

†Āpastamba (-dharmasūtra)—ii., 6, 14, 2 (34), 14 (12), 15 (12).

Uddyotana*—38.

Kavasha—50.

Kātyāyana—5, 10, 16, 17, 18 (2), 26, 28 (2), 29, 31 (2), 33, 34, 40, 43, 44, 46, 47, 48, 49, 50 (2), 51, 55.

†Gautama—xviii., 1 (2), 2 (2), 39 (12), 42 (14), 43 (14, 20).

Devala—6, 14, 17, 19, 28, 34, 38, 46, 47, 49, 50.

†Nārada—xiii., 1 (1), 2 (1, 44), 3 (1), 4 (2), 7 (45), 10 (30), 11 (29), 12 (8, 10), 16 (1), 18 (24), 26 (42, 55), 32 (18), 34 (11), 42 (42), 50 (35), 52 (39, 42).

Pāraskara—45.

Pitāmaha—33, 40.

Paiṭhīnasi—11.

Prajāpati—3, 33, 39, 40.

Bṛhaspati—1, 3 (from S. čandrikā), 5 (2), 7, 8, 9, 10 (2), 12, 15 (2), 16, 17, 19, 20, 21 (2), 22, 26, 27 (2), 29, 31 (2), 32 (anon.) 33 (2), 35, 39, 40 (4), 44, 51, 54, 55 (2).

†Baudhāyana—i., 5, 1-3 (36). ii., 2, 23 (25), 24 (25), 25 (26), 27 (11).

" Doubtful—26, 37.

Brāhmaṇa (a)—45.

Bhāradvāja—43.

†Manu—iii., 49 (41). viii., 416 (6). ix., 104 (6), 112 (2), 118 (10), 127 (23), 128 (23), 130 (35, 36), 131 (44), 133 (35, 36), 134 (26), 135 (48), 136 (35), 139 (36), 141 (23), 142 (23), 152 (18), 153 (18), 154 (20), 155 (20), 157 (19), 158 (25), 160 (26), 164 (25), 168 (23), 169 (23), 170 (23), 171 (23), 172 (23), 173 (23), 174 (23), 175 (25), 177 (23), 178 (25), 179 (21), 180 (25), 182 (27), 185 (38, 39), 187 (34), 192 (43), 193 (43), 194 (45), 195 (46), 196 (46), 197 (47), 198 (45), 200 (49), 201 (13), 202 (13), 203 (13), 204 (30), 205 (30), 207 (12), 208 (29), 210 (52), 211 (52), 212 (52), 214 (12), 217 (36, 40), 219 (30).

Manu doubtful—6, 39 (this is really Yajñ. ii., 142!)

" Bṛhan—37.

" Vṛddha—21, 28, 33, 40, 50.

Yama—48.

---

*Uddyota is quoted by the Dāyabhāga (II., 9) see Colebrooke's note where various guesses are contrasted.

†Yājñavalkya—ii., 112 (15), 114 (4), 115 (9), 116 (8, 12), 118 (29), 119 (28), 120 (15), 121 (4), 124 (11), 127 (22), 129 (24), 133 (21), 134 (21), 135 (34, 38, 40), 136 (34), 137 (56), 138 (53), 139 (40, 54), 140 (13), 143 (45), 144 (48), 147 (49), 148 (9, 49).

†Vasishṭha—xvii., 14 (24).

" doubtful—26, 31.

" Vṛddha—28.

†Vishṇu—xv., 40 (31). xvii., 3 (15), 4 (32, 33), 15 (56), 16 (56).

Vishṇu doubtful (? verse recension)—4.

" " (prose)—10, 19 (3), 29, 30.

Veda (Black Yajur)—6, 41.

Vyāsa—3, 4, 5, 31, 39.

Vyākhyātṛ (commentator)—52.

Çabarasvāmin (?)—6.

Çaṅkha—28.

" and Likhita—2, 9, 10, 12, 38.

Smṛiti—11, 18, 55.

" čandrika—3.

Hārīta—2, 7, 27.*

As regards the quotations from books which no longer exist except so far as they are cited by the authors of digests. it is necessary to observe that the difference in the texts is often very great, and especially between the Bengal and Southern works. The quotations in the Southern digests also differ more or less in each one. Partly this is to be attributed to the proverbial carelessness of the Pandits in such matters, but I think that most probably different recensions of the originals also existed; at least there are strong reasons for believing this as regards the metrical redactions of Kātyāyana and Bṛhaspati. Kārikās or diffuse metrical versions of scientific treatises have always been in great favor in India,‡ and have un-

* In the case of those marked † the quotations have been traced in the original, and the number of chapter and verse is given and that of the page in ( ). As the other books quoted are not in existence, I have given the page where they occur in the following translation, and the second number in ( ) gives the number of quotations on the page if more than one.

‡ It is remarkable that this was the case also in Rome, cfr. *Schöll*, "Legis duodecim tabularum reliquiae," p. 4 (etiam in metricam formam aliquando xii. tabulas falsas redactas—). We know from Megasthenes (ed. Schwanbeck, pp. 91 and 113) that in India there were formerly no *written* laws, and Strabo writing much later asserts the same fact (ed. Meineke iii., 991). It is therefore impossible that great differences should not have existed in the texts.

questionably promoted inaccuracy to a large extent. This is however a question that cannot be entered on here.

In the present translation I have adopted the versions usually consulted in the Courts where such exist. Thus I have when the Mānava-dharmaçāstra is quoted, taken that by Sir W. Jones. It is far from exact, and is elegant rather than critical, but I see little chance of a better translation being made. For Apastamba, Gautama, Nārada, Baudhāyana, Vasishṭha and Vishṇu I have used the excellent edition and translation of Dr. Bühler (in West and Bühler's Digest) which forms a sound foundation for practical purposes, and on which it would be difficult to improve.

I have however enclosed in brackets ( ) words which do not actually occur in the original. For practical men to interpret texts, they must know the bare contents; loose paraphrastic versions can but mislead.

For this reason I have not cared to make a readable translation. If Hindu Law ever becomes an object of interest, I have no doubt that some-one will be able to dress up my literal transcript of the original, and pass it off as an independent and new translation.*

For this version I used a Grantha MS. of about 1700 and very correct; I had a collation made of Tanjore No. 530, and found scarcely a single variant; I think therefore that in this case I have been able to represent the original nearer than has as yet been done in perhaps any similar work, for the MSS. of Sanskrit law-books seldom agree very closely.

Ootacamund, 28th May 1872. **A. B.**

---

* The original text should always be printed with translations like the present. Had a fount of Devanāgarī type been available, I would have done so, though it would necessarily add to the amount of loss certainly incurred by this publication.

LIST OF ABBREVIATIONS.

Bühler.	*West* and *Bühler's* Digest. Bombay, 1867-9.
C.	*Colebrooke.*
C. & CC.	Commentary or Commentaries.
D. & Digest.	translated by *Colebrooke*. 2 vols. 8vo. Madras, 1865.
Dāyavibhāga	Madras, 1868. By the translator.
J.	*Sir W. Jones.*
J. V.	*Jīmūtavāhana*. Calcutta Edition, 4° (with 7 *CC.*) and *Colebrooke's* translation in *Stokes* "Hindu Law Books," Madras 1865.
lit.	literally.
Manu	Ed. *Haughton*. 1825. I have also referred to the Bombay lithographed edition with *Kullūka's C.*
Mit.	Mitāxarā. Calcutta, 1829; Bombay (lith.) and *Colebrooke's* translation in *Stokes* "Hindu Law Books."
S. C.	Smṛticandrikā. MS.
S. V.	Sarasvatīvilāsa. MS.
Strange.	"Hindu Law" by *Sir T. Strange*, 3rd Ed. Madras, 1859. The Appendix is quoted as ii.
V. C.	Vivādacintāmaṇi, 8vo. Calcutta, 1837.
V. M.	Vīramitrodaya, 4° Calcutta, 1815.
Vyav. M.	Vyavahāra-mayūkha, MS. and Bombay lithographed Edition of ç. 1785, also *Borradaile's* translation in *Stokes* H. L. Books.
Yājñ.	Yājñavalkya, ed. *Stenzler*.

p. 87.

VARADARĀJA

ON

PARTITION AND SUCCESSION

I. Partition and Succession of Sons etc.

Occasions of partition.

The topic of law called partition of heritage is (next) explained; in regard to this Nārada (says xiii., 1):—

"Where a division of the paternal estate is instituted by sons, that becomes a topic of litigation called by the wise 'partition of heritage'." C.

In regard to this Vishṇu says (xvii., 1):—

If a father make a partition with his sons, (he does so) in regard to (his) self-acquired property at his own pleasure." (Bühler.)

As regards the topic—"the sons should divide" (Nārada xiii., 2) Nārada (says xiii., 3):—

"When the mother's menses have ceased, and the sisters have been married, or when cohabitation has ceased, and the father's sensual passions are extinguished, (then let the sons divide the estate)." C.

(xiii., 16):—

"A father who is afflicted with disease, or influenced by wrath, or whose mind is influenced by a beloved object, or who acts otherwise than the law permits, has no power in the distribution of the estate." C.

Bṛhaspati (says):—

"In default of both parents, partition of (i. e. by) brothers is indicated;

and though both parents be living, it is ordered (to be done) when the mother's menses have ceased."*

Çaṅkha and Likhita (say) in regard to this:—

"(Partition is directed), even though the father do not consent, if he be old, (or) of perverted intellect, and if he be afflicted with chronic (lit. long) disease."†

Gautama (also says xxviii., 1. 2):—

"After the father's death, let the sons (alone) divide the property (left by him). 2. (Let them also make a division) during the father's lifetime, if he wishes it, and the mother's menses have ceased." (Bühler.)

In regard to this Hārīta (says):—

"While alive also let him after making a partition, become a hermit, or let him enter the order of the old (i. e. fourth order), or let him having separated his sons by (giving them) a small portion live (by himself) taking the greater (part). If (however) he be reduced, he may again take (the property) from these (sons); and he may separate the reduced.‡

Now in regard to this (people) adduce (as an illustration) a vedic text about the refilling on exhaustion of the sacrificial jars:—

'The father is the āgrayaṇa, the sons are the other jars; if the āgrayaṇa be exhausted or should it dry up, one should take (Soma juice) from the other jars. § (So from the āgrayaṇa), if the other jars be emptied.' Thus it is explained."

In regard to this (says) Nārada (xiii., 4*a*):—

"Or the father, being advanced in years, may himself separate his sons."

C. By these and the like sayings a partition effected by the father and sometimes one by the sons is allowed; so also the

---

* D No. cxv.

† Cf. D. No. xvii. quite different from the above. J. V. i. 42. As in most cases where J. V. differs from the Mitāxarā, there is a difference in the original texts. See the remarks on p. xviii. of the preface

‡ D. xxiii. "Separate the reduced" Colebrooke translates:—"He must give a portion to sons reduced to indigence." The Sanskṛt idiom has—"Divide by (means of) a share." The whole of this passage including the illustration occurs in the Smṛti-čandrikā and the text of Hārīta is partially quoted in V. C. p. 127.

§ Kāty. Çr. S. ix., 5, 21. "Sāvitrapātnīvatabhāriyojanopaxīṇān āgrayaṇāt." Āp. xiii. and xiv. contain several notices of this practice in the Soma ritual.

time of partition is allowed at various periods. (Thus) one (1) time (is) when the father desires partition; (2) again if a father be alive but without desire and the mother's menses have ceased, even if the father do not wish it, partition (may take place) by the will of the sons. So again (3) though the mother's menses have not ceased, and though the father do not desire it, if the sisters have been given away (in marriage) and if the father be vicious or afflicted with chronic disease, partition occurs by will of (his) sons. So again (4) another time is after the father's decease."*

Prajāpati says that partition is to be made in order to the increase of dharma.

"So they may live together, or separately out of regard for dharma. (If they be) separate, dharma increases; therefore separation is right."

Bṛhaspati (as quoted) in the *Candrikā* (says):—

"The worship of pitṛs, devas and brahmans of (i.e. by) those living by one cooking (of food) would be single, (but) of divided persons that would occur in each (separate) house."

Vyāsa (says):—

"Of undivided brothers there is one dharma, but if partition occur, dharma would be separate for (each of) them."†

---

* Jīmūtavāhana (as indeed follows from his notions respecting the right of property) allows only two periods of division: during the father's lifetime by his will; and after the father's death. This view is criticized in the Vīramitrodaya (cf. 169 b. etc.). D. & S. V. follow J. V. The Mitāxarā is followed by the Mādhavīya (§§ 5 & 6), Smṛticandrikā, Virādacintāmaṇi (?), Vīramitrodaya.

The older writers do not however specify 4 times for division though their teaching in effect is the same as that of the later compilers who do so, most likely because of the controversy with the followers of J. V. (i., §§ 39—41) who evidently intends his arguments to be taken as against Vijñāneçvara's teaching in the Mitāxarā.

In Madras (1 High Court R. 77) partition may be enforced by a father, son, grandson or great grandson, but only in case of ancestral property.

† D. xiii.

So **Vyāsa** (also says):—

"During the both parents' lives, the brothers are directed to dwell together; (but) their d h a r m a increases when separated in their (the parents') default."*

Yājñavalkya says (ii., 114):—

Unequal partition.

If the father makes partition, he may separate his sons at his (own) pleasure; or (he may separate) the eldest with a best portion, or all may share alike."

C. When the father desires to make a partition, then he may separate (his sons) by his own will. (The share may be) equal or even unequal, for his will is uncontrolled. (**Yājñavalkya**) mentions an alternative—"or the eldest."

So **Manu** (ix., 112) says:—

"Of the eldest a twentieth (is the share) and what is best of all the wealth; let a half of that be (the share) of the middlemost, and a fourth of the youngest."

(Thus) by the method declared by **Manu** partition is to be effected (by giving) the eldest a best portion, the middlemost a middling portion, and the youngest a least portion. (**Yājñavalkya** then) states the established conclusion—"or all may share alike." In this (text) unequal partition refers to self-acquired property. As the father and sons have equally property in hereditary wealth, unequal partition by (the father's) will is not proper (in that case).

Partition of property inherited from a grandfather etc.

Yājñavalkya says (ii., 121):—

"Land acquired by the grandfather, a fixed allowance, or even wealth,—in that the property of both the father and son is alike."

So also **Vishṇu** (says):—

"In houses and fields inherited (from the grandfather and ancestors) the father and sons are equal sharers; but in (regard to) the paternal (property)

* J V. iii., 8.

(i. e. acquired by the father) sons cannot have partition against the father's will." *

Bṛhaspati (says):—

"In property both movable and immovable acquired by the grandfather, equal shares have been pronounced for both the father and son."

So also Vishṇu says (xvii., 2):—

"But in regard to the wealth of the paternal grandfather, the ownership of father and son, is equal." (Bühler.)

Kātyāyana (says):—

"Let the property of the paternal grandfather be common to both the father and son; in (the case of) self-acquired property (acquired) by the father, the son has no ownership."

So Vyāsa (says):—

"Property belonging to the paternal grandfather (which) had been taken away (but) which has been re-acquired by the father by his own power, (and property which) has been obtained by knowledge, heroism etc., the father's ownership in that has been stated (by the Smṛti). Out of that wealth he may make a gift, or even consume it at his will. In his default however (his) sons are declared to be equal sharers."

Bṛhaspati (says):—

"Of immovable property and also bipeds (slaves) though self-acquired, without having made all (his) sons partakers (in these articles), there is not gift nor sale (by the father")."

An exception to this (is made by the text):—

"Even one (member of a family) may give, pledge or sell immovable property in times of distress for the sake of the family, and especially for dharma sake. Of the jewels coral and pearls, of all (of them is) the father the lord, but of the immovable (property) neither the father nor the paternal grandfather." †

* This text is Vishṇu xvii., 1—2, turned into a Çloka, and is therefore probably from the Vishṇusmṛti in verse to which I am unable to refer.

† This text is nearly everywhere anonymous. Its origin has not been found out. The second sentence is quoted in the (Mādhavīya) Dāyavibhāga (§ 4. p. 5.) as a separate text.

By these and similar sayings it is inferred that sons and sons' sons have equal right to a paternal grandfathers' (property, but) that the father is independent as regards (his) self-acquired property.

But as for the two verses of Manu (viii, 416 and ix., 104):—

"(Three persons) a wife, a son, and a slave are (declared by law) to have (*in general*) no wealth (exclusively their own): the wealth which they may earn, (is *regularly*) acquired for the man to whom they (belong)." (J.)

"After the death of the father and the mother the brothers being assembled, may divide (among themselves) the paternal (*and maternal*) estate; but they have no power over it while (their parents) live (*unless the father choose to distribute it*). (J.)"*

And as for this saying of Devala.

"After the father is dead, the sons may divide the wealth of the father, for they would have no ownership were the father (alive) without fault."

These and the like (sayings which) go to prove a want of independence do not prove a want of property (as) the venerable Commentator (Çabarasvâmin) has said in (his discussion of) the topic—

"Aitiçaya (thinks) men are intended, because of the indication of sex." (Jaimini-sûtra, vi., 1, 6.)

So also a Vedic text says (B. Y. V. vi., 2, 1, 1.):—

"The wife indeed rules the household goods."†

So Manu says (?):—

"While both (the parents) are living, they be not independent, though (the father) be affected with old age."

---

*Sir W. Jones has omitted an important word 'Samam.' The translation should run—"may divide equally among etc."

†The only C. accessible to me as far as this part of the B. Y. V. is concerned is Bhaṭṭa Bhâskara's Jñânayajña which says—"patnī. . . . . īçe"—īçe iṣṭe, "Lopas ta âtmanêpadeshv" iti (Pāṇ vii, 1. 41) talopaḥ. hi ĉe 'tiṅighâtâbhâvaḥ. anudâttetvât lasârvadhâtukânudâttatvam. paritas sarvato sahyate badhyata iti pariṇad gṛham ucyate—etc. cf Schleicher, Indo G. Chrestom p. 57. (s. v. īç).

So Hārīta also (says):—

"While the father is alive the sons have no independence as regards giving or relinquishing property or fines."

Moreover—If (one consider) ownership (to exist) before (division, the word—) "he may divide" is required in all the Smṛtis; or, (if we consider that) ownership does not exist before partition it should be said—"he may give to his sons." Now (lit. thus) if ownership (arise) from partition, as a single son after (the death of) his father and mother does not (divide) the property, there would not be ownership; therefore by entry into the family (i. e. birth), there is certainly ownership (of the son) even in his fathers and grandfather's property.

Thus also Bṛhaspati (says):—

"Beings born, those to be born (but yet) in the womb, and those (still) in their father, all desire that subsistence, they are not to be deprived of it."*

C. The words "in the womb" are a qualification of "those to be born." Those produced in the form of sesamum or beans, and which are intimately connected with men who eat (those seeds) are said to be—"in their father"; after a while, being there ripened in the form of seed, and entering into a woman by connection with her are called "in the womb." So these have a right of ownership in their (fathers and mothers) wealth commencing with the connection of their parents, and then there is partition of (already) existing property, and not a right of property (arising) from partition. Therefore in the case of self-acquired property of the father, (there is) partition by (his) will, because of the superiority of the acquirer. In the case of inherited property there is partition by will of the father, and also by will of the son.

---

* J. V. I., 45. Both editions quote this as a text of Manu. The 7 CC. throw no light on the meaning. M. I., 1, 27. to same effect only.

In regard to partition of self-acquired (property) Nārada says (xiii., 15):—

"For such as have been separated by their father with an equal, less or greater allotment of wealth, that is a lawful distribution; for the father is the lord of all." (C.)*

So also Bṛhaspati (says):—

"(By these) when shares have been arranged by (their) father, (whether they be) equal, less or greater, they are to be preserved so, otherwise (if they disturb this arrangement, they) are to be punished."

Yājñavalkya says (ii., 116*b*.):—

"A partition by lesser or greater shares made by the father is said to be according to law."

But though unequal partition is thus seen in the Çastra, yet, as it is detested by people, it is not to be done, because of the prohibition—"what is detested by people is not conducive to heaven, and though legal, one should not do it."

And thus Prajāpati (says):—

"Just as the practice of appointing a (widow) woman, or the Anūbandhya (sacrifice) do not (exist any longer) so also partition by (unequal) shares does not take place."†

C. As the practice of appointment after the death of a husband is not carried out, because people detest it, or as the sacrifice of a cow (is no longer made), so the practice of unequal partition, though it be legal, because people dislike it, is not to be carried out in the Kaliyuga.

Partition during the father's lifetime.

Nārada mentions a special case on occasion of partition by a living (father, xiii., 12):—

"Let the father making a partition reserve two shares for himself." (C.)

---

* Slightly modified. My MSS. read—"samanyūnādhikair dhanaih"—for hīnādhikasamair dhanaih" as Dr. Bühler's text reads and Colebrooke's must have done. C. has—"an equal, greater or less allotment."

† This text is quoted in the (Mādhavīya) Dāya-vibhāga (§ 9. p. 10) and the argument is there the same as that used here. The authorship of the passage is there however ascribed to the compiler of the Saṅgraha.

So also Bṛhaspati (says):—

"Let a father on (making) a partition during his (life) take a couple of shares for himself."

And so also Çaṅkha and Likhita (say):—

"If he have (only) one son, let him take two shares for himself, and of slaves and cattle the best. A bull (is) the extra (portion) for the eldest." *

The fathers taking two shares refers to inherited property.

Shares of wives etc.

So some (say that this occurs) on separation with wives.

Yājñavalkya (ii., 115) says:—

"If (the father) makes an equal partition, his wives are to get equal shares, who had no Strīdhana given (them) by (their) husband or by (their) father-in-law."

C. When (the father) by his own will, makes all his sons sharers by equal (shares), then (his) wives of the same caste are to have equal shares with the sons; (namely) those wives to whom Strīdhana had not been given by the husband or father-in-law. If Strīdhana was given them (their) shares are to be made up having regard to that, as it has been thus declared with reference to Adhivedana (ii., 148).

"To a woman whose husband has married again, (the husband) should give equal Adhivedana, if Strīdhana has not been given her. If it has, he should make it a half." †

In this (verse) the word "half" is indicative (of the amount); therefore the meaning is that the share should be made up, having regard to what was given before. Having thus declared equality of shares for mothers on (occasion of) partition

---

* *D.* xliv., *C.* translates — "If there be one son, let *the father* himself reserve it." The MSS. read — "Sa (i.e. pitā) yady ekaputraḥ syāt", which I translate as above, because the topic under discussion is division by a father, and ekaputraḥ must be therefore a Bahuvrīhi compound. *C.* follows Jīmūtavāhana ii., § 59. The above translation is approved by the Smṛticandrikā.

† In Stenzler's text — "datte tv ardham prakīrtitam"; here the MSS. have — "datte tv ardham prakalpayet."

during the (father's) life, he (Yājñavalkya) also says that they get equal shares (on partition) after the father is dead (ii., 123).

"When (sons) divide after (their) father's death, the mother also should get an equal share."

So too Nārada (says xiii., 12):—

"The mother shall receive an equal share, if the sons divide after her husband's death." (C).*

Bṛhaspati (says):—

"But in his default the mother of sons gets an equal share."

Vyāsa (says):—

"Childless wives of the father are declared (to be) equal sharers, and grandmothers; they all are declared to be equal to mothers."

C. That is, it is right to give even a grandmother an equal share as (is done) in the case of mothers.

In regard to this Vishṇu (says):—

"Mothers and unmarried daughters take shares according to the shares of sons."†

So also Bṛhaspati (says):—

"Their mothers (have) equal shares, and the maidens fourth-part shares."

Kātyāyana says:—

"For maidens not given (in marriage) a fourth part is wished; three shares are for the brothers, but equality of distribution has been recollected in the case of property of small amount."

In regard to this Manu (says ix., 118):—

"To the unmarried daughters (*by the same mother*) let their brothers give portions out of their own allotments respectively, (*according to the classes of the several mothers*); (let each give) a fourth part of his own distinct share; so they who refuse to give it, shall be degraded." (J.)‡

Çaṅkha and Likhita (say):—

"When the heritage etc. is being divided, the maiden takes the maiden's ornaments and the marriage Strīdhana."

---

* My MSS. have dhave instead of the patau of *Dr. Bühler's* text, an irregular form to save the metre.

† Not in *Dr. Bühler's* text.

‡ "Unmarried daughters"—lit. "maidens." "Those who refuse to do so, shall be degraded"—lit. "Let those who do not desire to give, be degraded."

"Maiden's ornaments"—ornaments fit for a maiden.

So also Paiṭhīnasi (says):—

"The maiden gets the maiden's wedding ornaments (kanyāvaivahikam) and Strīdhana."

Baudhāyana (says):—

"The daughters shall inherit (of) the mother's ornaments as many as (are worn) according to the custom of the caste (Bühler, p. 318). Or something else." *

Vyāsa (says) in regard to this:—

"Those among them who have not been initiated, they are to be also initiated out of the paternal wealth by (their) eldest brothers, and the maidens also according to rule."

Nārada (says) in regard to this (xiii., 34):—

"If no wealth of the father exist, the ceremonies must be, without fail, defrayed by brothers already initiated, contributing funds out of their own portions." (C.) †

Yājñavalkya (says ii., 124):—

"Those who have not been initiated, shall be initiated by the brothers previously initiated; sisters also (must be married, the brothers) having given a fourth part (of a brother's share) from their shares."

The learned say that the ceremonies of marriage of daughters are obligatory, because mentioned in all Smṛtis, and that therefore the ceremonies also ending with marriage are to be performed by the elder sons previously initiated.

In this case, some (assert) that sufficient wealth for the ceremonies of the daughters is to be given (and) nothing else; but others are minded that a fourth part of a son's share should be given if there be much wealth, but that if there be (but) little wealth an equal share should be given. ‡

---

* The last part does not occur in *Bühler's* text.

† My MSS. here read avaçyakāryāḥ.

‡ The old traveller v. Linschoten (c. 1583) knew of the principle of Hindu Law as regards daughters. He says (p. 20? of the Calcutta reprint)—"but the sonnes inherite all, but they keep up and maintaine their daughters and sisters till they marry." "And they give no household-stuff with their daughters, but only jewels, and pay the charges of the wedding. The sonnes inherite all their goods."

Case of one who does not want a share.

Next; (Manu) has mentioned the partition of one who does not desire (a share), having given him something (ix., 207):—

"If any one of the brethren has a competence from his own occupation, and wants not the property (*of his brother*), he may debar himself from his own share, some trifle being given him as a consideration (*to prevent future strife*)." (J.)*

Yājñavalkya says (ii., 116):—

He who is able (to support himself) and wishes for nothing (of the father's property), may be separated by giving him something." .

Āpastamba says (ii., 6, 2, 14 & 15):—

"Therefore all who are virtuous inherit. But him, who expends money unrighteously, he should disinherit, though he be the eldest son." (Bühler).

Gautama says (xxviii., 39):—

"According to the opinion of some (lawyers) the son of a woman of equal caste even does not inherit if he be living unrighteously." (Bühler).

The partition of such is to be made having given them something (such as) betel etc. which forms part (of the property).†

Excluded heirs.

Next; Manu declares those who are unworthy of heritage (ix., 214):—

"All (those) brothers, (who are) addicted to (any) vice, lose their title to the inheritance" (J.)‡

Çaṅkha and Likhita (say):—

"Of one degraded, the inheritance, (funeral) cake and water cease."§

Bṛhaspati (says):—

"Though born of (a wife of) the same caste, one (who) has no (good) quality (is) not worthy of the paternal property. That (property) is said to belong to the Çrotriyas, who offer the cake for him (i.e. for the deceased father). A son saves his father from the highest and lowest debts;

---

* "He may debar himself" — lit. "he is to be debarred."

† i.e. Antatogatatāmbūlādi — v. l. antato gatvā — "having gone to the end (or finished the business of partition)."

‡ lit. "do not deserve wealth."

§ D. cccxviii.

hence there is no profit by heirs if perverse. What is the good of a cow which neither gives milk nor is (ever) pregnant? What is the good of a son (being) born who is neither learned nor righteous? But a son who is destitute of learning, bravery and wealth, (who) is void of devotion and discretion, (who) does not follow good custom, (such a son) is said to be no better (lit. equal to) urine and ordure."*

To such reprobates nothing whatever is to be given. However Manu says that they are to be maintained (ix., 201-3):—

"Eunuchs and outcasts, persons born blind or deaf, madmen, idiots, the dumb and such as have not the use of a limb, are excluded from a share of the heritage."†

"But it is just, that the heir who knows his duty, should give all of them food and raiment (*for life*) without stint, according to the best of his power. He who gives them nothing sinks assuredly to a region of punishment." ‡

"If the eunuch and the rest should at any time desire to marry, (*and if the wife of the eunuch should raise up a son to him by a man legally appointed*), that son and the issue of such (*as have children*) shall be capable of inheriting." (J.)

Yâjñavalkya says (ii., 140):—

"A eunuch, (or) one degraded (and his) offspring, one lame, a lunatic, (or one who is) an idiot, one blind, one afflicted with incurable disease and similar persons, are to be maintained though they do not get portions." §

"Their Aurasa or Xetraja sons, if blameless, get shares, and their daughters are to be maintained, until they are married."

"And their childless women (who) behave well are to be supported; (if) adulterous, they are to be expelled; so also, (if) obstinate."

C. "Degraded"—the murderer of a Brahman etc. "His offspring"—the son of a murderer of a Brahman. "A lunatic"—one troubled by madness; marked by attacks consequent on disorders of the aerial, bilious and phlegmatic

---

* D. cccxix.

† The word in the text is nirindriyāh — Rāghavānanda in his C. explains it — "Such as have not the use of a limb are n. Deprived of a hand etc."

‡ Better: "But food and clothing without stint is to be given to all (of them) by a wise man, as he can; for one not giving (them such food and clothing) would be degraded."

§ The MSS. here read tu instead of the syuh of *Stenzler's* text.

humours, or on a mixture of them. "An idiot"—one whose power of perception is disturbed, who is not able to distinguish between good and bad. They do not get shares if afflicted before partition, but (this does) not (apply) to one (already) separated. The "Aurasa and Xetraja sons" of these (i. e.) "the eunuchs etc." if free from the defects which prevent (them from) taking shares, do (however) get shares. The Xetraja son is (that) of the eunuch. The others also have Aurasa sons. In consequence of the Aurasa and Xetraja sons both getting shares there is neglect of the other sons. The "daughters" of the eunuch etc. are to be "maintained" (i. e.) they are to be supported till they are married. "The childless women" of those (namely) the eunuch etc. if they (the women) "behave well" are to be maintained; otherwise, "if adulterous, they are to be expelled".

Devala (says):—

"Though the father be dead (sons who are) eunuchs, lepers, insane, idiots or blind, one degraded, the offspring of a degraded (son), one who bears a sign, (these) do not get shares."

"To them, except to the degraded, food and clothes is (to be) given. Their sons (if) free from defects should take (their) father's share of the heritage."

C. The offspring of a degraded person, by reason of his having a defect because of the degradation, has nothing to do with the heritage.

Vaçishṭha (says):—

"But (brothers) who have entered a different order (i. e. have become Vanaprasthas or Yatis) as well as (those who) are eunuchs, madmen, or out-casts, receive no share. Eunuchs and madmen are entitled to maintenance" (Bühler.)

Gautama (says xxviii., 42, 3):—

"An idiot and an eunuch (should be supported).—42. The (male) issue of an idiot receives the share of his father." (Bühler.)

Case of sons born after partition.

Now in the case of divided and undivided persons **Manu** (ix., 216) has declared the succession by one who is undivided to the wealth.

"A son born after a division (*in the lifetime of his father*), shall (alone) inherit the patrimony, or shall have a share of it with (the divided brethren, if) they return and unite themselves with him." (J.)

Bṛhaspati (says):—

"If there are uterine brothers born of fellow wives (and) who have been separated by (their) father, their younger brothers succeed to the father's property. Having given (separate) purificatory ablutions (after his death) they are mutually incompetent (to inherit)."

Yājñavalkya (ii., 112) says that for one born after partition (a provision of) a share is to be made from (the divided brothers') own shares if there be no property of the father.

"After the partition, if a son be born of a woman of the same caste (as the father) he gets a share; or let his share be from the visible property gain and loss."

Vishṇu (says xvii., 3):—

"(Sons) who have separated from their father should give a share to (a brother) born after partition. (Bühler.)"

Partition of sons and grandsons.

Next; **Yājñavalkya** mentions partition between a grandson and son (ii., 121):—

"Land acquired by the paternal grandfather, a fixed allowance or even wealth; in that the property of both the father and son is alike."

Bṛhaspati (says):—

"A debt, a field, a house, a bond belonging to a paternal grandfather, in those one who has been absent for a long time gets a share."

C. Because the paternal grandfather's property belongs equally to both father and son.

Yājñavalkya has declared that the partition is thus, if several sons of one man having begotten sons even or uneven in number either (still) are alive or are dead (ii., 122):—

"Of (heirs) by several fathers, the arrangement of the heritage is according to fathers."

C. That is sons' sons get shares through their fathers.

Bṛhaspati (says):—

"What has been gained by all together, in that all have equal shares. Their sons (whether) equal or unequal (in number) are declared (to be) takers of their father's shares."

C. What has been gained "by all together" (i. e.) not divided, by agriculture etc. that even though gained by one (such member of the family) is common to all. Their sons (whether) equal or unequal (in number) certainly take (their) father's shares.

Kātyāyana also mentions a peculiarity in regard to this:—

"If a younger brother die undivided, one should make his son a sharer (if) he had received no inheritance from his paternal grandfather.

"He should receive his father's share from his paternal uncle, or from his (the uncle's) son; let that be the share of all the brothers according to law."

"Let his (i. e. the grandson's) son take that (i. e. in default of his father)." Beyond let there be a cessation." *

C. An undivided brother being dead, one should make his son who has not received subsistence from his father, a sharer in the wealth. His share in the wealth (is) his own father's share. (If) the paternal grandfather be dead, (he gets it) from the paternal uncle by partition. If the paternal uncle be dead, he gets his share by partition from his son; but on partition, from (his) paternal uncle's son the share (for him) should be that which would be for the brothers according to law. This is said:—

"Brother's sons whether equal or unequal in number take their father's shares."

If one of the former (i. e. brothers) dies, his son the fourth (in succession from the paternal grandfather) certainly takes (a share). There is a cessation commencing with the fifth as there is a want of Sapiṇḍaship (on his part).

---

* D. lxxix.

Devala however says that there is a cessation with the fourth:—

"The rule (is) that a partition again between undivided and divided (but re-united) members of a family living together (extends) to the fourth (in descent).

"So far members of a family would be Sapiṇḍas; beyond, the funeral cake is said to cease. (The learned) will that the partition of heritage and the funeral cakes correspond. This rule has been proclaimed for brothers of the same caste. If there be only a single (one) of the same caste the heritage is not divided."

C. There is again partition as far as the fourth of members of a family who though (onee) divided have reunited. Beyond that there is no partition of heritage, for the reason that they are not Sapiṇḍas. If there be Sapiṇḍaship, there is a partition of heritage; therefore as the fifth is not a Sapiṇḍa there is not a partition.

The rule for brothers born (of wives) of the same caste has thus been explained, but not (the rule) for those born of women of different eastes (to the father).

Kātyāyana also in stating that for brothers born of women of the same caste there is not in equality of shares, because they are of one easte, has pronounced a cessation of partition beyond the fourth:—

"Having discharged obligations, let him divide the rest. But so that property is to be taken in order by his sons as far as the fourth (in deseent)."

C. By the word "obligation" a debt is meant.

It is to be observed that if the father, grandfather and great grandfather be dead, there is Sapiṇḍaship as far as the fourth male (in descent) previously spoken of. Because of the Sapiṇḍaship of the three former, if they be alive, Sapiṇḍaship is limited to seven men (in descent). With that opinion **Bṛhaspati** says:—

"He who is the third, fifth or even seventh of his descendants, when he returns, the land is to be given him by the Gotrajas."*

*Cf. D. cccxciv., 4.

In that case Nārada has declared that there is partition of shares (lit. heritage) out of what is left (after discharge) of debts and (performance of) ceremonies (xiii., 32):—

"What remains of the paternal inheritance over and above the father's obligations, and after payment of his debts, may be divided by the brethren; so that their father continue not a debtor."* (C.)

C. By the word "father's obligations" the funeral rite of the father etc. is intended.

So Kātyāyana (says):—

"The debt incurred (lit. made) by the brother, uncle or mother on account of the family, all that is surely to be paid at the time of partition by the persons (who get) the property."

Division of the residue.

Now in regard to the succession to the property after (discharge of) debts and (performance of rites, Prajāpati (says):—

"Let the visible (property), the house, land and cattle (lit. quadrupeds) be divided; in case of suspicion of concealed wealth, in that case the ordeal has been declared."

In this case a distinction (arises) from another smṛti.

"On partition of a house (the share) of the eldest is at the southern part (of the house); and of the next the share is after him (i. e. the eldest brother), and so on of the rest."

Kātyāyana (says):—

"On partition of land, groves, houses, etc. taking place, let the southern part be the share of the eldest, or the western.

Case of sons by wives of different castes.

Next; Manu (ix., 152—3) mentions the partition of sons born of marriages (by women of different castes) in (the regular order of) succession:

"152 or, (*if no deduction be made,*) let some person learned in the law divide the whole (collected) estate into ten parts, and make a legal distribution by this (*following*) rule:

"153. Let the son of the Brāhmaṇī take four parts; the son of the

*The MSS. read—ṛṇī na syād yathā pitā. Dr. Bühler reads ṛṇī syād anyathā pitā—which is not supported by Colebrooke's translation.

Xatriyā three; let the son of the Vaiçyā have two parts; let the son of the Çūdrā take a single part, (*if he be virtuous*)." (J.)

Bṛhaspati (says):—

"Let Brahmans, Xatriyas, Vaiçyas and Çūdras begotten in order by a Brahman, be (heirs) by four, three, two and one share in succession. (Let) those begotten by a Xatriya (have) three, two and one (share); (let) those begotten by a Vaiçya have two and one share."

C. Let the Brahman woman's son born in the direct order (by marriage with a Brahman man get) four shares; the Xatriya woman's son, three shares, the Vaiçya woman's son born in the direct order (i. e. by marriage with a Brahman man), two shares; but the son of a Çūdra woman, a single share. So the son of a Xatriya by a Xatriya woman (gets) three shares; the son of a Xatriya by a Vaiçya woman, two shares; the son of a Xatriya by a Çūdra woman (gets) one share. So (again) the son of a Vaiçya by a Vaiçya woman (gets) two shares; a Vaiçya's son by a Çūdra woman (gets) one share.

Manu (ix., 157) mentions a difference in regard to this:—

"For Çūdra is ordained a wife of his own caste, (*and*) no other. All produced by her, shall have equal shares, though she leaves a hundred sons." (J.)

Vishṇu (says) in regard to wives in every case:—

"Mothers take shares according to the share of the sons." *

"In every case an only son of a father, born in the direct order takes all the paternal wealth."—said Devala.

C. But let an only son (born) in the direct order get the entire wealth of his father.

This refers to (all) except the son born of a Çūdra woman. But Vishṇu states that an only son born of a Çūdra woman by a Brahman gets a half:—

"An only Çūdra son of twice born (men) is taker of a half. (That) which is the course of a childless man's (wealth), that also is (the course) of the half share."†

* Not in the published text.

† do. D. clxxii.

C. The meaning is that that half goes to the nearest Sapinḍas.

Devala mentions a difference:—

"But let a Nishāda (who is the) only son of a Brahman get two shares; let the Sapinḍa or Sakulya who performs the funeral rite (Svadhādātṛ) take the two (remaining)."*

C. In this case by the word "Nishada" one born of a Çūdra woman is meant. It is to be understood that the taking of a half or of a third (share refers) to a very obedient Çūdra (son).

Manu mentions a difference (ix., 154—5):—

"But whether (the Brahman) have sons, or have no sons, (*by wives of the three first classes*), no more than a tenth part must be given to the son of a Çūdra."†

"The son of a Brahman, a Xatriya, or a Vaiçya by a woman of the servile class, shall inherit no part of the estate (*unless he be virtuous, nonjointly with other sons unless his mother was lawfully married*). Whatever his father may give him, let that be his." (J.)

Bṛhaspati (says):—

"Let an obedient (son) of a man who has no (other) children, (if he be) possessed of good qualities (though he be) born of a Çūdra woman, get subsistence; let the Sapinḍas get the rest."‡

C. It must be held that such sayings as "The Çūdra woman's son does not get a share in the heritage" etc. which forbid (succession) to property, refer to a disobedient (son by a Çūdra woman).

Gautama (xxviii., 43) says that a father should give maintenance to sons born even in the inverted (order of castes), such as Sūtas etc. who live with him, and are obedient.

---

* D. clxv.

† Lit. "One should not, according to law, give to the son of a Çūdrā (i.e. Çūdra woman) more than a tenth."

‡ D. clxviii.

"(The sons begotten) on women of higher classes (by low class men) are to be treated as sons begotten (by a Brahman) on a Çūdra wife." (Bühler.)

Land, Brahmadāya etc. go to Brahman son only.

Bṛhaspati mentions a difference:—

"Land got by acceptance is not to be given to a son of a Xatriya woman etc.; if the father give it him, when (the father) is dead, let the Brahman woman's son take it."*

C. (When) the father "is dead" let the Brahman son alone "take it".

So Vṛddha Manu mentions a difference in the case of brahmadāya (i. e. what has been gained by a Brahman in virtue of priestly functions etc.):—

"Let the Brahman woman's sons take land descended as brahmadāya, (but let) all twice born (sons take) the house and land."†

C. There is (here) cessation (of heritage) to the son of the Çūdra woman, because the twice born (sons) get (the property).

Bṛhaspati (says):—

"A son born of a Çūdra woman by a twice born man deserves not a share of the land; the law is established that a twice born (son) should get it all."‡

Case of a son by a dāsī.

Next; Manu mentions a difference in regard to (a son) born of a dāsī § (ix., 179):—

"But a son, begotten by a man of the servile class on (his) female slave, or on the female slave of (his) male slave, may take a share of the heritage, if permitted (*by the other sons*): thus is the law established." (J.)

So also Yājñavalkya (ii., 133. 4):—

"(A son), though begotten on a dāsī by a Çūdra, may take a share at will. When the father is dead the brothers should make him a sharer by half (a share)".

---

* D. clxi. † D. clx. ‡ D. clxiv.

§ I have already (Dāyavibhāga, p. xiv. note) mentioned that 'female slave' is hardly an adequate translation of dāsī. Now-a-days only a devadāsī or temple prostitute can be understood.

C. In every case it must be understood that the succession of a dāsī's son to the property (is) in default of ordinary or excellent sons, sons' sons, daughter's sons etc., because of what is said from—"(a son) though begotten on a dāsī by a Çūdra" to—"if he has no brother, he may take all, except there be daughter's sons." (ii., 134).

12 kinds of sons. Next; in order to explain the succession of the twelve kinds of sons Manu defines them (ix., 166. 7).

"Heirs whom a man has begotten on his own wedded wife, let him know (to be) the first in rank (as) the son of his body."

"He, who was begotten, according to law, on the wife of a man deceased, or impotent, or disordered, after due authority given to her, is called the lawful son of the wife." (J.)

Yājñavalkya (ii., 127):—

"A son (who is) begotten by a childless man on another man's wife with permission, he according to law inherits the property of both, and presents the piṇḍa (for them)."

C. This (son) has double sonship by:—

"The son born from seed is of the owner of the seed; the Xetraja is said (to be the property) of the owner of the field."

C. And so, on partition, as his double sonship is recognized, he is a dvyāmushyāyana; (but) as he gets his proper share from his natural father, it must be understood that he is superior to a Xetraja (son).

In regard to this Bṛhaspati (says):

"Having sacrificed to Agni and Prajāpati it is done as has been said by Gautama, others however say that a childless man's daughter is be considered (as his son)."*

(It is said) in another smṛti:—

---

*Cf. D. ii., p. 355 (Text not numbered). "Gautama has said, (that a daughter is appointed) after making an oblation to fire, and performing the sacrifice called prājāpatī (or prājapatya); but others hold, that a (girl who was) supposed (to be a son whilst in her mother's womb), is an appointed daughter."

"Some say that an appointed daughter (is so) only by (special) agreement."

Vasishtha (says xvii., 1. 12):—

"I shall give thee (to the husband) a brotherless damsel, decked with ornaments; the son whom she may bear, be he my son." * (Bühler).

Manu (ix., 127. 8):—

"He, who has no son, may appoint his daughter in this manner to raise up a son for him, *saying*, "the male child, who shall he born from her in wedlock, shall be mine for the purpose of performing my obsequies.

In this manner Daxa himself, lord of created beings, anciently appointed all his fifty daughters to raise up sons for him for the sake of multiplying his race." (J.)

In this case then there are two sons: the (appointed) daughter is (in the place of) a son, (which is) one (kind); and the appointed daughter's son is the other.

Manu (ix., 168):—

"He whom his father, or mother (*with her husband's assent*), gives to another as his son, provided that the donee has no issue, if the boy be of the same class and affectionately disposed, is considered as a son given, (*the gift being confirmed*) by (*pouring*) water." (J).

Ditto. (141). Of the man, to whom a son had been given, (*according to a subsequent law*), adorned with every virtue, that son shall take (*a fifth or sixth part*) of the heritage, though brought from a different family." (J.)

Ditto. 142. "A given son must never claim the family and estate of his natural father: the funeral cake follows the family and estate; but of him who has given away his son, the funeral oblation is extinct." (J.)

Ditto. 174. "He is called a son bought, whom a man, for the sake of having a son (*to perform his obsequies*), purchases from his father and mother, whether the boy be equal or unequal (*to himself in good qualities, for in class all adopted sons must be equal*)." (J.)

Ditto. 177. "He, who has lost his parents, or been abandoned (by them) without just causes, and offers himself to a man (*as his son*), is called a son." (J.)

---

* The MSS. here read bhavishyati instead of the bhavad iti of Dr. Bühler's text. Perhaps the first reading is preferable, as there the text is complete if altered as a mantra.

C. "Offers himself" means gives himself.

Ditto 169. "He is considered as a son (*made or adopted*), whom a man takes as his own son, the boy being equal in class endued with filial virtue, acquainted with (*the*) merit (*of performing obsequies to his adoptor*), and with (*the*) sin (*of omitting them*)" (J.)

Ditto. 170. "In whose mansion soever a male child shall be brought forth (*by a married woman, whose husband has long been absent*), if the real father cannot be discovered, (*but if it be probable that he was of an equal class*) that child belongs to the lord of the unfaithful wife and is called a son of concealed birth in his mansion." (J.)

Ditto. 171. "A boy, whom a man receives as his own son, after he has been deserted (*without just cause*) by his parents, or by either of them, (*if one be dead*), is called a son rejected." (J.)

Ditto. 172. "A son whom the daughter of any man privately brings forth in the house of her father, if she (*afterwards*) marry her lover, is described as a son begotten on an unmarried girl." (J.)

Yājñavalkya (ii., 129):—

"A Kānīna born of an unmarried (maiden) is reckoned as a son of his maternal grandfather."

Nārada (xiii., 18):—

"Let the damsel's son, born through his mother's folly (born of his mother by a secret person), whose father is unknown, present funeral oblations to the father of his mother, and inherit his property."* (Bühler).

C. If there be a person to marry her, the damsel's son belongs to the husband; if there be not, or if (the father) be unknown, he is (his) maternal grandfather's son.

Vasishtha (xvii., 14):—

"If an unmarried daughter bear a son (begotten) by a man of equal caste, the maternal grandfather has a son through him; he shall offer their funeral cake and take the wealth (of the grandfather)." (Bühler).

Manu (ix., 173):—

"If a pregnant young woman marry, whether her pregnancy be known

---

*The MSS. read — gūḍhamātṛjaḥ — born of (his) mother by a secret (person). Dr. Bühler has corrected the text as above on the authority of the V. M. the MSS. also read — hareta saḥ.

or unknown, the male child in her womb belongs to the bridegroom, and is called a son received with his bride." (J.)

(*Do.* 175.) "He, whom a woman, either forsaken by her lord, or a widow, conceived by a second husband, whom she took by her own desire, (*though against law*), is called the son of a woman twice married." (J.)

(*Do.* 178.) "A son, begotten through lust on a Çûdrâ by a man of the priestly class, is even as a corpse, though alive, and is thence called (in law) a living corpse." (J.)

C. "Though alive"—is certainly a living corpse.

(*Do.* 180.) "These eleven sons (the son of the wife, and the rest as enumerated) are allowed by wise legistators to be substitutes (*in order*) for the sons of the body, for the sake of preventing a failure of obsequies.' (J.)

(*Do.* 158.) "Of the twelve sons of men, whom Manu sprung from the Self-existent has named, six are kinsmen and heirs; six, not heirs, (*except to their own fathers*), but kinsmen." (J.)

Baudhâyana has said (ii., 2. 23, 24) that the first six share the heritage, (but) the last six belong to the family. As in this matter in all the smṛtis the order of the sons is recited differently, one should neglect the order and make a partition among the six, according to circumstances. Hence it is said:—

"In default of a better a worse (one) gets a share."

C. He who is best by birth is "a better."

"An Aurasa, a daughter's son, a Xetraja, a Datta (or) Kritrima, a gûḍhaja, and an apaviddha (the learned) say get shares. They say also that a Kânîna, a Sahoḍhaja, a Krîta, also a Paunarbhava, a Svayamdatta and a Nishâda belong to the family." (Baudh. ii., 2. 20.)

Some (authorities) state that the Aurasa and Xetraja are the most excellent.

"The Aurasa and Xetraja sons both share their father's wealth. The ten others in order get a share of the family wealth."

C. By "a share of the (family) wealth" subsistence only is intended.

Manu (ix., 164) has declared the rule for the share of a Xetraja.

"The Aurasa dividing his father's heritage, should give a sixth part of the paternal wealth (as) the Xetraja's share, or a fifth."

In regard to this Bṛhaspati (says):—

"A single Aurasa is declared owner of (his) father's wealth."

"A daughter's son is said to be equal to him; the rest, it is recollected (i. e. said by some person on authority of the Veda) should be supported."

In regard to this (says) Manu (ix., 134 and 160):—

"But, a daughter having been appointed to produce a son for her father, and a son, (*begotten by himself*), being afterwards born, the division of the heritage must in that case be equal; since there is no right of primogeniture for a woman."

"The son of a young woman *(unmarried)*, the son of a pregnant bride, a son bought, a son by a twice-married woman, a son self-given, and a son by a Çūdrā, are the six kinsmen, but not heirs (*to collaterals*)." (J.)

By these sayings, six inherit from their relatives (bandhu); the others get food and clothing.

Vasishṭha mentions a difference in regard to this:—

"If after he has been received, an Aurasa be born, let him have a fourth part." *

C. A reception of a Datta (son) having taken place, on the birth (after that event) of an Aurasa, let the Datta get a fourth part from the Aurasa. This refers to much property.

Kātyāyana (says):—

"After an Aurasa son has been born, sons of the same caste take a third part; but those not of the same caste get food and clothing." †

So also Baudhāyana:—

"All those sons are recollected to be heirs of a man who has no Aurasa (son); if however an Aurasa be born, primogeniture does not rest with them. Their sons of the same caste get a third part; let those who are deprived (hīna) live on him (the Aurasa), being furnished with food and clothing." ‡

---

* Not in the printed text of Dr. Bühler.

† D. ccxviii.

‡ Not in the printed text. This seems to be taken from a verse recension as yet unknown.

Why enlarge (on this topic)? Some (say) that this (text):—

"The Aurasa son alone is lord of (his) father's wealth; he should however give them maintenance for blamelessness' sake"—

is only in praise of an Aurasa (son).

Bṛhaspati (says):—

"(Of) the twelve sons who were mentioned in succession by Manu, of these the Aurasa and likewise the Putrikā continue the family. As, if there be no butter, oil is admitted by the wise (as) a substitute (at sacrifices); so are the eleven sons (admitted as substitutes) if there be no Aurasa or Putrikā."*

In this case Manu has mentioned an extension of the application of (the term) son (ix., 182):—

"If, among several brothers of the whole blood, one have a son born, Manu pronounces them all fathers of a male child by means of that son; *(so that, if such nephew would be the heir, the uncles have no power to adopt sons).*" (J.)†

Hārīta (says):—

"If, of many brothers begotten by one (father), one have a son, there is no doubt that they all have sons in him (lit. by that son). If, of many wives of one man, one have a son all obtain by that son the position of (wives) with sons."

Manu has thus directed (that such a child is a) substitute (for a son); but (that he) is not a substitute is held by Hārīta, by reason of (his) words:—

"All obtain by that son the position of (wives) with sons."

Bṛhaspati (says):—

"If (there be) many uterine brothers begotten by one man, if a son is born to one (of them), they all are recollected to have sons. Of many wives of one man that rule is recollected; if one of them has a son he presents the piṇḍa for all of them."

The learned hold that the meaning of the sayings which indicate an extension of application of (the term) son is, that, funeral ceremonies are to be performed by them.

---

*I have corrected this text as it occurs in Vaidyanātha's treatise on Çrāddhas. The MSS. have "thirteen sons not mentioned by Manu."

†One MS. here adds the next text by Hārīta.

Expense of funeral ceremonies.

Next (is to be considered) the fee for (performing) ceremonies.*

Devala (says):—

"Now if the performer of the ceremony requires a fee, he may take a tenth, or a fifth part of the dead man's wealth, or even all."

Kātyāyana (says):—

"If any other than the son, pupil and uterine (brother) burns (the corpse), if he require (a fee) he may take a tenth part, a fifth, or even all (the property). Çaunaka (says) that he may take the tenth part of a wealthy man's (estate), the fifth of a poor man's, and the estate of one who leaves neither son, father or wife."

"If any other than the son, pupil or brother burn (the corpse) he may for this (act) take (his) fee, a thousand, a hundred or fifty cows."

Vṛddha-Vasiṣṭha (says):—

"He may burn (the corpse of) a Sapiṇḍa, or (of) one who is not a Sapiṇḍa, or (of) the priest of wealthy men."

Impartible property.

Vṛddha-Manu mentions what is impartible:—

"What is a man's wealth (gained) by learning, let that be his; a friendly gift, marriage presents (are his own exclusive property); also what belongs to a madhuparka."†

In regard to this Yājñavalkya (says) (ii., 119):—

"He who gets back property inherited in due course (but which) has been taken away, should not give that to heirs; also what he has gained by learning."

Çaṅkha even (directs) that in regard to immovable (property).

"He who if alone recovers in order land formerly lost, having given him a fourth the others get their share "‡

Kātyāyana (says):—

"What has been obtained by bravery and by learning, also what is called Strīdhana, all that on partition is not partible; (it is) of the owner. On no account is (anything) to be given by a learned man to unlearned (members of his family); but that wealth is to be given by a learned man to (those who) have equal or greater learning."§

---

*Cfr. the commentary on D. clxv.

†A madhuparka is a nasty mess said to be presented on certain occasions. See the Prayogaratna (article on marriage).

‡D. ccclix.

§D. cccl. The first sentence does not occur here.

Nārada (says) (xiii., 11):—

"A learned man needs not give a share of his own acquired wealth without his assent, to a learned coheir: provided it were not gained by him, using the paternal estate."* (C.)

(*Do.* 6):—

"Both what is gained by valour, and the wealth of a wife, and what is acquired by science, these are three sorts of property exempt from partition; and any favour conferred by the father." (C.)†

(*Do.* 7):—

"And if the mother has given through affection (a portion of) her (separate) property to one (of her sons), to that also this (the above rule) refers; for the mother is like the father (able to bestow gifts)." (Bühler.)‡

Yājñavalkya (ii., 118):—

"What else is self-acquired (by an heir) without prejudice to the father's wealth, a friendly gift, and a marriage gift, that does not belong to the heirs."

(*Do.* 123, 4):—

"Property which has been given by the father and mother to any one (child) let that be his."

Bṛhaspati (says):—

"What has been given by the grandfather and father, and by the mother, is not to be taken from him; so also wealth (gained by) heroism and a wife's wealth."

Manu (ix., 208) and **Vishṇu**§:—

"What a brother has acquired by labour or skill, without using the patrimony, he shall not give up without his assent; for it was gained by his own exertion." (J.)

Kātyāyana:—

"(If) learning has been acquired by the expenditure of (wealth) enjoyed by a stranger, (or) from anywhere else (i. e. not at home); that (which is) gained legally by this learning, is called "wealth acquired by learning."

---

*In the last half of the Çloka, my MSS. read pitṛdravyam. This reading does not affect the sense.

†The MSS. here read—avibhājyāni.

‡The MSS. here read—mātā 'pi 'bhṭo tathā pitā.

§No such text appears in the published text of Vishṇu.

"What has been gained by knowledge on a wager with a stake, one should know that to be 'wealth (acquired) by learning'; it is not divided on partition."

"(And) what has been obtained from a pupil, from (officiating in) the office of a ṛtvij (i.e. a priest at a sacrifice), for (answering) a question, for settling a difficult question, for display of knowledge, for a disputation, and for excellence in reciting (the Vedas etc.), (the learned) have pronounced that (to be) 'wealth acquired by learning,' it is not divided on partition."

This rule also (applies) to constructive arts* and what is (gained) above the cost price.†

"And also a paṇa‡ given for learning, and what is got from a sacrificer, or from a pupil; (the learned) have pronounced this 'wealth acquired by learning'. What (is acquired) otherwise than by this, is common."

"One should know that (wealth) which is brought by a wife is 'marriage wealth' (vaivāhika). All such wealth is to be recognised as a means to duty."

Manu (ix., 219) and **Vishṇu**§ (say):—

"Apparel, carriages, or riding horses, and ornaments, (*of ordinary value, which any of the heirs had used by consent before partition*), dressed rice, water (*in a well or cistern*), female slaves, family priests, or spiritual counsellors, and pasture ground for cattle, the wise have declared indivisible, (*and still to be used as before*)." (J.)

Nārada (says) (xiii., 10):—

"He who maintains the family of a brother studying science, shall take, be he ever so ignorant, a share of the wealth gained by science." (C.)¶

Manu (ix., 204-5):—

"After the death of the father, if the eldest brother acquire (*wealth by his own efforts before partition*), a share of that (*acquisition*) shall go to the younger brothers, if they have made a due progress in learning; and if all of them, being unlearned, acquire property (*before partition*) by their own

---

*Çilpa, i.e. architecture, sculpture, painting and constructive arts.

†This seems to mean the gain, through the application of skilled labour, over and above the cost price of the raw materials.

‡A small copper coin = in value 80 Couries. Hence our fanam, and the Tamil word for money.

§This Çloka is not in the published text.

¶The MSS. support Dr. Bühler's emendation of this Çloka.

labour, there shall be an equal division of that property (*without regard to the first-born*); for it was not the wealth of their father: this rule is clearly settled." (J.)

Vasishṭha:—

"And if any of them have self-acquired property let him take two shares."*

Vyāsa (says):—

"The wealth (a brother) acquires by heroism etc. having used a chariot or weapon which is common property, in it (his brothers have shares). To him (the acquirer) a double portion is to be given; the rest share equally."

Next **Kātyāyana** mentions partible (wealth):—

"The grand-father's and father's (wealth) also and what else is self-acquired, on partition between the heirs, all that is divided."

"Having given property for return gift, the rest should be divided. That is to be taken (i. e. shared) as far as the fourth in order, also, by their (the heirs') sons."†

Bṛhaspati:—

"Household furniture, beasts of burden, cows, ornaments (and) slaves when found (visible) are divided; in (the case of) concealed (property) the ordeal is prescribed."‡

Kātyāyana:—

"Bṛhaspati says that the (self-acquired) wealth of brothers educated in the family or by the father, and what they (i. e. such brothers) gain by heroism is to be divided."§

Therefore partition is to be made by sons and sons' sons. Bṛhaspati makes a distinction in regard to this:—

Performance of obsequies.

"One should set aside sedulously from the given (i. e. existing) property, a half or the half of that, for the monthly, Shāṇmāsika (half-yearly) or for the yearly Çrāddha."

Vishṇu (xv., 40):—

"And he who takes the wealth is recollected (to be) "the presentor of the funeral oblation."‖

---

*Not in the published text. †D. ccclviii — ix.

‡D. ccclxxiv, where it is attributed to Kātyāyana. C. has "household utensils."

§D. ccexlix. ‖Slightly altered from Dr. Bühler's text. The MSS. read piṇḍadaḥ for piṇḍadāyī and insert Smṛtaḥ.

C. Whoever (as heir) gets a man's property, he should perform the Çraddha for him (from whom he inherits). That is to say, after getting (it), he should present (the funeral cakes) for three persons.

"Having taken the movable, the immovable (property) the gold, silver, grain, liquids, (and) clothes, one should cause to be performed the monthly, Shāṇmāsika (half yearly) and yearly Çrāddhas."†

C. One should present at the Çraddha, the grain, seats, clothes, umbrellas, shoes and rings even. The rest of the property is to be divided.

(ii. Order of Succession in default of Sons.)

1\. Wife (widow). The wife is declared to inherit on default of sons. In regard to this Vishṇu (xvii., 4. flg.) (says):—

4.) "The wealth of man who dies without male issue goes to his wife."‡

5.) "On failure of her to his daughters."

6.) "On failure of her, to his father."

7.) "On failure of him, to his mother."

8.) "On failure of her, to his brother."

9.) "On failure of him, to his brother's son."

10.) "On failure of him, to the (relations called) Bandhu."

11.) "On failure of them, to the (relations called) Sakulya."§

12.) "On failure of them, to a fellow-student."

13.) On failure of him, it goes to the king, with the exception of a Brahman's property."‖

14.) "Let those who are Brahmans take a Brahman's property."¶

---

†D. cccxcix attributed to Bṛhaspati.

‡The MSS. read anapatyasya pramitasya dhanam for apatradhanam of the printed text.

§The MSS. invert the Sûtras 11, 10.

‖The MSS. have brāhmaṇadhanavarjam.

¶The MSS. here read—brāhmaṇadhanam brāhmaṇā ye' vagṛhiṇīyuḥ; the printed text—brāhmaṇārtho brāhmaṇānām; both being to the same effect.

In regard to this Bṛhaspati (says):—

"Of a man deceased without (leaving) sons (his) wife is to be recognised as heir, or (his) mother, or brother by his permission."

Vṛddha Manu (says):—

"A wife (widow) who has no sons, keeping the bed of her husband unviolated (and) firm in duty, should indeed offer the funeral cake and take the whole share."*

Prajāpati:—

"In tradition (i.e. the Vedas), in the smṛti-doctrine, and by (lit. in) popular usage, the wife is declared by the wise to be half the body (of her husband) equally (sharing) in the fruit of good and bad acts."

"Of him whose wife is not deceased, half his body survives; how should another take the property, while half (his) body lives?"†

Bṛhaspati:—

"The widow (wife) is recollected (as) succeeding to her husband's wealth; in her default, the daughters; in their default the brother's sons, the Sakulyas and also Bāndhavas."

Kātyāyana:—

"Now of a childless man the widow (wife) born in the (same) caste, or the daughters; in their default the father, mother, brother and sons are proclaimed (heirs)."

Pitāmaha:—

"Though there be kulyas and uterine brothers of the father, the widow (lit. wife) succeeds to the property of (a man) deceased without offspring."

Bṛhaspati:—

"Let the (wife) deceased before (her husband) take (i.e. be burned with) the (sacred) fire; let her who survives (her husband) take the wealth."‡

"Should her Sapiṇḍas or Bāndhavas and her enemies injure the property, let the king punish them with the punishment (decreed) for a thief."§

* D. cccviii.

† Do. cccxcix. These verses are there assigned to Bṛhaspati.

‡ D. cccxcix. v., 4. Vyav. M. iv., viii., 2. The MSS. have all many vv. ll.

The Bombay lithographed Vyav. M. (f. 39) and a MS. read pūrvam mṛtā tv agnihotram mṛte bhartari taddhanam | labhet pativratā nārī dharma esha sanātanaḥ.

§ D. cccxvi. "Those near or distant kinsmen, who becoming her opponents, injure etc", tatsapiṇḍāḥ — her or his (the deceased's) Sapiṇḍas.

In regard to this Yājñavalkya (ii., 135—6) says:—

"The wife, the daughters also, both parents, the brothers, their sons, gotrajas, a bandhu, a pupil and a fellow-pupil."

"In default of a former, the next in succession gets the property of one deceased without offspring. This (is) the rule for all castes."

C. The woman who has been married, who is subdued (and) is endowed with (the merit of) sacrifices should take the whole wealth of a childless man who has been separated, (but) has not been reunited. If there be many (women) of the same and different castes (to the husband) having divided (the property), they take according to shares.

Vyāsa has mentioned a distinction:—

"Heritage also to the amount of two thousand (paṇas) is to be given to a woman (wife) out of the wealth; and what wealth has been given (her) husband, let her have that as she likes."

C. If (property) has not been given (her), two thousand paṇas are to be taken by the wife, not more. In default of the wife the unmarried daughter may get (it);—(thus says) Kātyāyana:—

"A wife, if she be not adulterous, takes the property of (her) husband; but in (her) default, a daughter if she be then unmarried."

Devala:—

"And paternal property is to be given to maidens, (viz, enough) wealth for marriage ceremonies. A legally begotten daughter may, like a son, take the property of a (father deceased) without a son".

(There is) Sapiṇḍaship of an unmarried (daughter) by Manu's text (ix., 187. a):—

"To the nearest Sapiṇḍa (male or female), after him (in the third degree) the inheritance next belongs—" (J.)

and that the Sapiṇḍa succeeds to the wealth is inferred from Āpastamba's text (ii., 14—2):—

"On failure of sons the nearest Sapiṇḍa (takes the inheritance)." (Bühler.)

In default of an unmarried (daughter), it is to be taken by a married (daughter) though not a Sapiṇḍa.

In regard to this **Manu** and **Nārada** (say):—

(**Manu ix.,** 130):—

"The son of a man is even as himself, and as the son, such is the daughter (*thus appointed*): how then (*if he have no son*), can any inherit his property, but a daughter, who is closely united with his own soul?" (J.)

Nārada (xiii., 50):—

"On failure of the son, the daughter inherits, for she equally continues the lineage, a son and a daughter both equally continue the race of their father." (C. and Bühler.)*

Bṛhaspati (says):—

"The wife (i. e. widow) gets the property of (her) husband, in her default, the daughter is recollected (as heir). A daughter, like a son, springs from each member of a man: how then should any other mortal take the father's wealth?"

Daughter's son.

In default of daughters **Vishṇu** directs that daughter's sons shall succeed.

"In the case of a man (deceased) without son, son's son or lineage, let the daughter's sons take the property. In performing funeral rites for ancestors, daughter's sons are esteemed (equal to) son's sons."†

C. In default of son's sons, what is to be done by son's sons is to be actively done by daughter's sons; and so **Manu** (ix., 130) says:—

"The son of a man is even as himself and as the son, such is the daughter (*thus appointed*): how then (*if he have no son*), can any inherit his property, but a daughter, who is closely united with his own soul?"

136. "By that male child, whom a daughter thus appointed, either by an implied intention or by a plain declaration, shall produce from a husband of an equal class, the maternal grandfather becomes in-law father of a son: let that son give the funeral cake and preserve the inheritance.

133. "Since their father and mother, both sprang from the body of the same man, between a son's son and the son of *such* a daughter, there is no difference in law."‡ (J. altered.)

* The MSS. read — tulyasantānadarçanāt.

† This quotation is from a verse recension of Vishṇu.

‡ The half Çlokas are here inverted.

139. *b.* "For even the son of such a daughter delivers him in the next (world) like the son of his son." (J.)

130. *a.* "The son of a man is even as himself; and as the son, such is the daughter." (J.)

133. *b.* "Between a son's son and the son of *such* a daughter, there is no difference in law." (J.)

Parents. In their default both parents take the wealth.

And so Manu (iv., 217. a) says:—

"On a son (dying) childless (*and having no widow*) the (father and) mother shall take the estate." (J.)

Brothers. In default of both parents, brothers succeed to the property. Now of brothers, uterine (brothers) should first take.

Devala (says):—

"Therefore the uterine (brothers) should divide the heritage of a (brother deceased) without a son." (But Manu said as above).—

"The mother shall take the estate." (How then) should the uterine (brothers) divide (it)?

(These) two texts do not refer to the order (of succession), but merely refer to the authority to succeed to the property. (There is) no contradiction. In default of uterine (brothers), their sons share the wealth. In default of both of them (i. e. in default of uterine brothers and of uterine brothers' sons), brothers by different mothers and their sons (succeed). In default of brothers' sons, their sons (i. e. brothers' sons' sons) succeed. After them, as there is want of Sapiṇḍaship, Samānodakas and Gotrajas succeed to the property.

Samānodakas. And so (says) Baudhâyana (Pr. I. 5, 1—3):—

"The great grand father, the grand father, the father, one's own uterine brothers of the same caste, the son of a (wife) of the same caste, a sons' son, (and) his son, and his son; and amongst these they call a son and sons' son Sapiṇḍas who share in an undivided oblation. The sharers of divided oblations they call also Sakulyas.

"Though sons be living, the property (of a deceased male) descends to these (i. e. first the sons and next the other Sapiṇḍas)."

Sakulyas. "On failure of Sapiṇḍas, a Sakulya (inherits)."*

C. i. e. the above mentioned Sapiṇḍaship, if the father, father's father and father's father's father be alive, (extends) even to the three former. Sapiṇḍaship extends to seven males†; so also Bṛhan Manu (says):—

"Sapiṇḍaship ceases with the seventh male, but the relationship of Samānodaka should cease with the fourteenth."

He also mentions another rule:—

"As far as there is recollection of birth (say) some; beyond that (it is called) gotra."

Sagotras. In default of Samānodakas, Sagotras succeed to the property. Bāndhavas (succeed) in default of Sagotras.

Bandhu. Baudhāyana says that these Bāndhavas are of three kinds:—

"(1) One's own father's sister's sons, one's own mother's sister's sons, and one's own maternal uncle's sons are to be known (to be) one's own Bāndhavas. (2) A father's father's sister's sons, a father's mother's sister's sons, a father's maternal uncle's son are to be known (to be) a father's Bāndhavas. (3) A mother's father's sister's sons, a mother's mother's sister's sons, and sons of a mother's maternal uncle are to be known (to be) a mother's Bāndhavas."‡

Pupil etc. In default of Bāndhavas a pupil succeeds. In default of a pupil a fellow-student. In his default any Çrotriya Brahman whosoever

*Cfr. Dr. Bühler's text which differs much.

†Cfr. p. 17, and J. V. xi. i. § 38.

‡This text does not occur in the printed text, but is in Çlokas and perhaps from a verse-recension. The V. M. Vyav. M. and S. V. say it is a Smṛti. It occurs in many Nibandhas, cfr. Dāyavibhāga § 41. V. C p. 155. Only 9 Bāndhavas are mentioned, but all other Sapiṇḍa relations who are not gotrajas also come in under this class, and inherit according to their nearness to the deceased. *Bühler*, pp. liv. & 176 — 8 (based on Mit. ii. v., 1 & V. M. f. 200, p. 21, 1. 6 (? f. 209 line 7). *Dr. Goldstucker's* argument ("On some Deficiencies etc." pp. 24 — 31) can leave on doubt no this point.

may take (the property). The king may take the property of Xatriyas etc. in default (of heirs) as far as a fellow-pupil. This is the succession of heritage in all castes. The Uddyotana and the Peerless* etc. are however of opinion that because of the word "certainly" (in the verse Manu, ix., 185)

"Not brothers, nor parents, but sons, (*if living, or their male issue*) are heirs to the deceased, but of him, who leaves no son, (*nor a wife, nor a daughter*), the father shall take the inheritence; and, (*if he leave neither father, nor mother*) *certainly* the brothers" (J. *who omits* 'certainly'.)—

that in default of sons the succession of brothers to the property first is intended. Now by Çankha and Likhita's text:—

"The property of one gone to heaven without (leaving) a son goes to the brother; in his default the mother and father should take (it), or the senior wife—"

it is also inferred that (the property) goes first to the brother.

So also by Devala's text:—

"Therefore the uterine (brothers) should divide the heritage of a (brother) deceased without (leaving) a son; the Sakulyas, or the daughter, or a father also (may do so); (or) brothers of the same caste, the mother and the wife in order. In their default the Kulyas who are sharers together—"

it is inferred that an uterine brother should in the first place get the wealth of a childless (brother deceased). Some say that in default of an uterine brother that the mother and father should get it. Others however assert that brothers by different mothers (should succeed). Others (again say that) one who is reunited (is meant). Others (say that) in default of those mentioned the wife (succeeds); for texts such as "the wife, the daughter," (Yājñ. ii., 135) and the like, which refer to a wife (i. e. widow) succeeding first to the wealth (of her deceased husband), all these (they say) refer to an appointed wife. Again the texts which give the property to daughters,

---

*The Uddyotana may be some C. It may however be a mistake for Uddyota which occurs in other treatises. "The Peerless" (Asahāya) is explained as meaning Medhātithi (author of a C. on the Mānava-dharmaçāstra); it may however be a proper name. Cfr. Mit i., vii 13.

these (they say) refer to a Putrika. Others say that women have nothing to do with inheritance by reason of the Vedic text:—

"Therefore women are powerless (and) do not get a share."

So (also) by Vyāsa's text:—

"Till death (maintenance) is to be taken before bathing (by the widow) in the community, despising beds, food and clothes, (her) husband being dead."

So (also) by the text:—

"Property was made for the sake of sacrifices; in them women have no authority; they all have no share in the wealth, they get only morsels (of food) and clothing.

So (also) by Nārada's text (xiii., 52):—

"Except in the case of Brahmans; but a king who is attentive to the obligations of duty, should give a maintenance to the women of such persons. The law of inheritance has thus been declared." (C.)

So (also) by Bṛhaspati's text:—

"If a widow be youthful and self-willed, even then a maintenance is to be given her to enable her to pass her life."

So by Manu's text*:—

"And their childless women (who are) well behaved are to be supported."

So by Prajāpati's text:—

"An āḍhaka (of rice) is to be given for "widow's food" to one who has lost (her) husband."†

And so also by the text:—

"For food a prastha of rice in the afternoon, together with fuel—" they consider that a widow who has not a son is to be merely supported by the kinsmen, but does not get heritage; but that the kinsmen succeed to the property. (We are of opinion that) this is entirely wrong. For in Manu's text (ix., 185, b):—

"But of him, who leaves no son, (*nor a wife, nor a daughter*), the father shall take the inheritance; and, (*if he leave neither father, nor mother*), *even* the brothers." (J. who has omitted *even*.)

---

*This is not in the Mānava-dharma-çāstra, but in Yājñ. ii., 142, a.

†Dāyavibhāga § 44.

there is no word to indicate the order (of succession), there is not disregard of the wife, but by the word "even" the brother's priority in regard to the father (is intended). So also in—

Manu's text (ix., 217, a):—

"Of a son, dying childless (*and leaving no widow*), the (*father and*) mother shall take the estate." (J.)

as there is no word having reference to the order (of succession), there is not disregard of the wife. Although by **Çaṅkha** and **Likhita's** and **Devala's** two texts (p. 38.) it is inferred that uterine brothers first suceeed to the property, yet by **Vishṇu's** text (xvii., 4):—

"The wealth of a man who dies without male issue goes to his wife." (Bühler.)

Also by **Bṛhaspati's** text:—

"A childless widow who preserves (chaste) the bed of her husband and who is firm in (her) duty, etc."

(So also) by **Vṛddha Manu's** text:—

"The wife takes her husband's wealth."

So by **Prajāpati's** text:—

"In tradition etc." (p. 38.)

So **Bṛhaspati's** text:—

"The wife succeeds to the husband's wealth, etc."

(So) by **Kātyāyana's** text:—

"Now (a wife) born of the (same) k u l a (succeeds to) the wealth of (a husband) who leaves no son."

By **Bṛhaspati's** texts:—

"The wife (succeeds) to (a husband) who leaves no son."

By **Pitāmaha's** text:—

"Though there be K u l y a s—"

By **Bṛhaspati's** text:—

"Of one deceased without a son."

And (by) **Yājñavalkya's** text:—

"The wife also the daughters (p. 34.)."

(Thus) by many texts (as above) the prior succession to all the wealth by a well conducted wife (i. e. widow) is inferred and (therefore) the explanation of the (above) two texts (of a different purport) is to be made in accordance with these.

The text:—

"The wealth of one deceased without a son goes to the brother."

means that the wealth goes to a reunited brother. Or, though there be a contradiction in the order (as far) as the reading (is concerned), the prior succession of the wife, the daughter and of the mother and father should be allowed, so that most (lit. many) texts do not contradict (one another). The statement that all the texts referring to the wife's heritage mean an appointed wife, is wrong; for in all of them an appointment is not mentioned. So also the statement that all the texts which refer to a daughter's succession mean a putrikā, is wrong; for the appointment of a daughter is not everywhere recommended. Again, as for the explanatory remark (in the Black Yajurveda).—"Therefore women are (nir indriya) powerless* (and) do not get a share"—that means that women do not get a share in the pātnīvata-graha; for we see that indriya means (sometimes) soma-juice.

"Indriya (means) soma drink. (B. Y. V. ii., 3, 2.)

Indriya (therefore) does not (here) mean strength (semen); for we see that women also have strength (Manu iii., 49. a):—

"But a boy (is in truth) produced by the greater quantity of the male strength; and a girl by a greater quantity of the female." (J.)

Thus one cannot say that "women are powerless". It is certain (lit. right, that) indriya (here) means soma.

(The text)—"Till death etc." (p. 39.)

*Cfr. p. 39. This is the conclusion to a story in B. Y. V. vi., 5, 8, 2. Varadarāja evidently follows Mādhava (Dāyavibhāga § 41). It is impossible (were it even of the least utility) to translate nirindriya by a word which would express all the different meanings of that term.

(refers to the case) when a husband with little wealth is deceased and (the widow's share) on partition is not sufficient for maintenance, then it is said (what) is sufficient for maintenance should be taken. Or this (same) text "till death etc." refers to an undivided husband.

(As for the text),—"Property was made for the sake of sacrifices" (p. 39.) the word sacrifice here is merely intended to indicate duty. For if sacrifice were only intended, it could not bear the meaning of gifts or homa. (But) as women do actually perform charitable acts, there is (thus) no contradiction.

That (the text):—

"Except in the case of Brahmans etc." (Nârada, xiii., 52 p. 39.)—

refers to secluded (i. e. kept women), is known from the subject-matter (of the context).

(The text):—

"If a widow be youthful etc." (p. 39.)

is intended to forbid that a (widow) suspected of adultery should take the whole wealth.

(The text):—

"Their childless women are to be supported." (p. 39.)—

it is clear from the subject-matter refers to the wives of eunuchs etc. There is (thus) no contradiction; for maintenance only is mentioned as they do not succeed to the property through their husbands.

Such texts as—"an âḍhaka (of rice) is to be given to (a wife) who has lost her husband" (p. 39.) and "for food a prastha of rice" (p. 39.) refer to women suspected of adultery.

As for Nârada's text (xii., 26, a):—

"Let the brothers allow a maintenance to his women for life" (C.)—

and (do. 42, a):—

"The property of reunited co-parceners is considered to be exclusively theirs" (C.)—

(these) refer only to the maintenance of the childless women of reunited (co-parceners whose case) is being discussed (where the texts occur). As for the texts of **Kātyāyana**:—

"When (one) who has been separated is dead in default of sons, the father should take the wealth."

"Or the brother, or the mother, or the mother of his father in due order."

they must be understood of (the case where there is) default of the (deceased's) wife and daughter. How can she, who during her husband's life shares with him in all the wealth, have nothing when he is dead? Therefore it is certainly correct that a well behaved wife takes all the wealth. Some however are of opinion that the texts (referring to) a wife's heritage refer to cases where there is but little property, and that where there is much property the kinsmen succeed.

Bhāradvāja (says) with reference to sons by a "punarbhū (wife):—

"Should two (sons) born of a woman by two (husbands) dispute about the wealth, what is the paternal wealth of each (of them) that let him take; not the rest."

C. The meaning is that they should take (each) his father's wealth.

Strīdhana.

Next; **Manu** (ix., 192) explains the partition of Strīdhana):—

"On the death of the mother let all the uterine brothers and uterine sisters (*if unmarried*) equally divide the paternal estate: (*each married sister shall have a fourth part of a brother's allotment*)." (J.)

C. An extra portion or uneven partition is not to be made as in the case of the father's wealth, but the partition of the uterine brothers (lit. males) and sisters (lit. women) is equal in the case of the mother's property.

He also mentions something else to be done (ix., 193):—

"Even to the daughters of those (daughters) it is fit, that something should be given from the assets of their maternal grandmother, on the score of natural affection." (J.)

Bṛhaspati makes a distinction:—

"Strīdhana (belongs) to the children, and the daughter if not betrothed has a share in it. Married (daughters) receive an honorary trifle."

Çankha and Likhita (say):—

"The uterine brothers and the maidens deserve equally all the mother's wealth."*

Gautama (xxviii., 21):—

"But a woman's separate property (Strīdhana) belongs (in the first instance) to her unmarried daughters, (and on failure of them), to those daughters who are poor." (Bühler.)

Vāsishṭha (xvii., 23):—

"Let the daughters divide the nuptial present of their mother." (Bühler.)†

Yājñavalkya (ii., 117, b):—

"The daughters should divide the (property) of the mother which remains after debts are paid. In default of them (i. e. daughters), the descendents."

C. In default of daughters, "the descendents," (i. e.) sons should take it, such is the meaning.

Nārada (xiii., 2, b):—

"Let daughters (divide the estate) of their mother (after her death), (or) on failure of daughters, their issue. (C.)

(C.) The meaning is that, if sons be well off, in default of daughters, their "issue" (i. e.) daughter's sons should succeed.

Kātyāyana says:—

"But in default of daughters, their property goes to their sons."‡

Manu (ix., 131, a):—

"Property given to the mother on her marriage (i. e. yautaka) is inherited by her *unmarried* daughter." (J.)

C. Yautaka is what is received (by the mother) from her family. That the daughters (share). In regard to Strīdhana received from the husband's family, the sons and daughters are equal because of (their) sapiṇḍaship. In

---

* D. cccclxxxviii. † Erroneously numbered 24 in the translation.

‡ D. ccccxcili., 1.

default of maiden (daughters), a (daughter) who is betrothed though not provided for, is equal with sons. "Not provided for"—who has no children, as (we learn) from a Brāhmaṇa:

"Offspring is a provision."

Or, (a daughter) if she be poor (is intended). In regard to this Manu makes a distinction (ix., 198):—

"If a widow (*whose husband had other wives of different classes*) shall have received wealth at any time (as a gift) from her father (*and shall die without issue*), it shall go to the daughter of the Brāhmaṇī wife, or to the issue of that daughter." (J.)

C. If wives (of other castes) than the Brāhmaṇa, be deceased without children, the maiden daughters of the Brāhmaṇi wife) should take their property, or her son; not the husband etc. This only refers to "Strīdhana given by the father."

In regard to this Pāraskara (says):—

"Strīdhana is said to belong to the daughter not betrothed; the son does not get (any thing); should (the daughter) be betrothed, however, (he) gets an equal share."

Next; Manu gives the definition of Strīdhana (ix., 194):—

"What was given before the nuptial fire, what was given on the bridal procession, what was given in token of love, and what was received from a brother, a mother, or a father, are considered as the six fold (separate) property of a *married* woman.' (J.)

In regard to this Nārada makes a distinction (xiii., 7):—

"What has been given before the nuptial fire, what was presented in the bridal procession, her husband's donation, or what has been given by her brother, mother or father, is termed the six fold property of a woman." (C.)*

Yājñavalkya (ii., 143):—

"What (a woman has had) given (her) by (her) father, mother, husband or brother, and what she has received at the marriage (before the fire), what she has received in her husband's marriage with another woman and the like, is called Strīdhana."

---

* The MSS. read bhrātṛdattam pitṛbhyām ca.

Vishṇu (says) (xvii., 18):—

"That which has been given to a woman by her father, mother, sons or brothers, that which she has received before the sacrificial fire (at the marriage ceremony), that which she receives on supersession, that which has been given to her by her relations, her fee and a gift subsequent, are called "woman's property" (Strīdhana). (Bühler.)

Devala (says):—

"Let the means of subsistence, the ornaments, the Çulka and gain be Strīdhana."*

Kātyāyana (says):—

"What wealth has been obtained by arts (by a wife), and what (has been given) by another out of affection, the husband has ownership there in the wealth; but let the rest be Strīdhana."†

"At the time of marriage what is given to a woman before the fire, that is said by the good to be "Strīdhana given before the fire."‡

"What moreover a woman gets while she is being conducted from her father's house is called "Procession Strīdhana."§

"Whatever is given out of affection either by the mother-in-law or father-in-law is called "Reverence Strīdhana."||

What is obtained by a woman from her husband's family after marriage, also what is obtained from (her) relations is called "Anvādheya Strīdhana."¶

"Whatever is obtained from household furniture, beasts of burthen, milch-cows, ornaments, or artizans, or cost-price, (that) is called Çulka."**

Manu says (ix., 195):—

"What the received, after marriage from the family of her husband, and what her affectionate lord may have given her, shall be inherited, even if she die in his lifetime, by her children." (J.)

He also makes a distinction (ix., 196).

C. The meaning is—after the five kinds of marriage mentioned (before by Manu) if the (wife be deceased) without offspring, the Strīdhana belongs to the husband.

---

*Cfr. D. cccclxxviii. †D. cccclxx. ‡D. cccclxiv.

§D. cccclxv. ||D. cccclxvi. ¶D. cccclxviii. 1.

**D. cccclxviii. 3.

(Manu ix., 197., also says):—

"But her wealth given on the marriage called āsura, or on either of the (*two*) others, is ordained, on her death without issue, to become the property of her father and mother. (J.)

C. The meaning is that Strīdhana given by the father and mother on occasion of three (forms of) marriage, (namely) the Āsura, Paiçāċa and Rāxasa, if the woman be deceased without offspring, belongs to the mother and father.

Devala (says):—

"Strīdhana is common (property) of the sons and maidens if the mother be dead. If she (be deceased) without offspring, the husband, mother, brother, or father should take it."*

C. By the first half (Çloka) it is stated that if the mother be deceased, sons and daughters take equally Strīdhana (got) by (any of) the eight forms of marriage; by the last half it is stated that the wealth got by the Āsura etc. three forms of marriage, is taken by those who gave it. The husband should take what he has given; what has been given by the mother etc. is to be taken certainly by them.

Kātyāyana (says):—

"But in default of daughters that wealth belongs to the sons. What has been given by bandhus, in default of bandhus goes to the husband. Let the sisters who have husbands divide (it) together with the bandhus. This rule has been ordered in the case of partition of "Strīdhana."†

C. "But in default of daughters" etc. refers to the eight (kinds) of marriage. "What has been given by bandhus" refers to the Āsura etc. marriage; in default of sons; what has been given by "bandhus"—maternal uncles etc., is to be taken by them. What has been given by bandhus, in default of such bandhus, goes to the husband. By "Let the sisters" he mentions an alternative; though there be bandhus, the sisters who have husbands

---

* D. cccclxxxix. mother—lit. woman. † D. ccccxciii.

should divide with the bandhus what has been given by bandhus.

Kātyāyana (also says):—

"What paternal (property) Strīdhana has been received by a woman on an Āsura etc. marriage, in default of her children, belongs to the mother and father."

Yama (says):—

"What property is given on āsura etc. marriages, if (the woman) be deceased without children, (her) father should certainly take (that) wealth."*

Gautama (xxviii., 2—34) (says):—

"The sister's fee belongs to her uterine brothers, if her mother be dead."

"Some say (that it belongs to them even) whilst the mother lives." (Bühler.) †

Yājñavalkya (says) (ii., 144):—

"What has been given by bandhus, likewise (her) Çulka, also (her) anvādheyika, if she be deceased without (having) children, the bandhus should get that."

C. Of these, the Çulka is of two kinds:—one, what is given to the possessors of a maiden by way of price for the sale of the maiden, (and) that goes to the mother, or to the brother. The other (kind of) Çulka (is) that, which is given for the ornaments of the maiden or for household furniture, and that is to be taken by the givers.

In regard to this **Manu** (ix., 135) (says):—

"Should a daughter, thus appointed to raise up a son for her father, die by any accident without a son, the husband of that daughter may without hesitation, possess himself of her property." (J.) ‡

In regard to this **Baudhāyana** (says):—

"The brothers should take equally the property of a deceased maiden; in their default it belongs to the mother; in her default it belongs to the father." ¶

---

* Cfr. D. DV. † Numbered in the translation 22 & 23.

‡ By any accident lit. anyhow. ¶ From some metrical recension.

Devala (says):—

"If a maiden be deceased, the brothers should take equally the property; in their default it belongs to the mother, or to the father's mother in order."

Manu (ix., 200):—

"Such ornamental apparel, as women wear during the lives of their husbands, the heirs of those husbands shall not divide among themselves, they who divide it among themselves fall deep (*into sin*)." (J.)

An exception is made by this (verse), as (otherwise) because the ornaments are not Strīdhana as they have not been given (to the wife), they are the property of the husband, and would therefore be divided by the sons on the husband's death. (The wife's) right to ornaments given out of affection being established, (next, to avoid the possibility of error), **Nārada** mentions an exception in the case of immovable property:—

"What has been given to a woman by an affectionate husband, that, though he be dead, she may consume or give away as she likes, except (what is) immovable."*

C. The meaning is, that, immovable (property) given out of affection is not the property of the woman, when the giver is dead. Some however assert that even immovable (property) given out of affection (is) the property (of the wife). They say that it is stated that—

"In absence of a (qualified) person to give his consent, it cannot be given away."

In regard to this **Yājñavalkya** (ii., 147) makes a distinction:—

"Strīdhana which a husband has taken in case of starvation, for a righteous purpose, in case of sickness, (or when) in prison, he need not give (back) except he likes."†

Kātyāyana (says):—

"Not the husband, nor even the son, not the father nor the brothers, have any power to take or give Strīdhana."

---

* Not in the printed text of ch. xiii. Dāyavibhāga § 50 (p. 42) also attributes this text to Nārada.

† The MSS. read nākāmo dātum. Stenzler reads—na striyai dātum.

"If any one of them consumes forcibly Strīdhana, he is to be caused to return it with interest, and is to get punishment."

"If he has been permitted to consume it in a friendly way, he is to be caused to return the value, if he be rich."

"But he should return voluntarily what has been relinquished for him out of affection (by the wife), knowing (that her husband is) sick, in distress, or oppressed by wealthy (creditors)."*

Devala (says):—

"Let food and clothes, ornaments, Çulka and gain be Strīdhana; the husband cannot consume all this of his own accord, if not in distress."

If he fraudulently give (it) away, or spend it, he should give (the value) to the woman with interest. He may use Strīdhana to remove the distress of a son."†

Kātyāyana:—

"A woman who is given to injurious acts, who is shameless and wastes the property, and who delights in adultery, does not deserve Strīdhana." "Strīdhana promised by the husband is, like a debt, to be paid by the sons; whether she (the widow) abide with her husband's family or with (her father's) family."‡

Vṛddha Manu (says):—

"What wealth has been received from (her) own husband except Çulka, that is Arhaṇa;‖ one may divide (this) remainder, but she (the wife) has certainly a share in it."

Kavasha:—

"The price for the sale of a damsel, or arhaṇa, or Çulka; one may divide that, but she certainly gets a share."§

Kātyāyana:—

"What has been received by a married (woman) or by a damsel, from

---

* D. cccclxxv. 4—7. † Do. cccclxxviii.

‡ D. cccclxxxiv. and cccclxxxiii. *C.* must have had a different reading of the last half verse which he translates:—"provided she remain with the family of her husband, but not if she live in the family of her father."

‖ A token of respect.

§ The MSS. have tadvināçam which must be an error for tadvibhāgam, as it gives no possible sense to the verse. I have therefore altered it as in the preceding text which is much the same.

(her) husband or in (her) father's house, or from (her) brother, or from both parents, that is called Sandāyika."

"Women's independence is stated in regard to Saudāyika they have acquired."

"Because that maintenance was given by these to quiet them, women's independence in regard to Sandāyika has always been proclaimed, both as regards sale or giving (it) away, and even in the case of immovable property."*

C. The meaning is that in time of distress although the husband, son, etc. have not given their consent, there is no blame if she sell or dispose of (such things).

Yājñavalkya (ii., 148):—

"To a woman who has been superseded (by a second marriage) he should give equal ādhivedanika, if strīdhana has not been given her. If it has been given her, he should make it a half."

C. Here the word "a half" means a complete share.

Kātyāyana:—

"Now if he have two wives, and if he does not still honor her (the first wife), he is to be made to give (her it back) even what she has relinquished (to him) through love."

"When a woman is deprived of food, clothing and house-room, in that case she may recover her property; so on partition of the heirs."

"This is an unvarying law relating to husbands. When she has got it, she should dwell in her father's house However if sick or at point (lit. time) of death, she may go from thence to her husband's house."†

Bṛhaspati makes a distinction in regard to this:—

"The mother's sister, the wife of a maternal uncle, a paternal uncle's wife (lit. woman), a father's sister, the mother of a wife, and an elder brother's wife are declared equal to a mother."

"If they have no Aurasa (son), an (other) son, nor a daughter's son, (nor) his son, their sister's sons etc. should take their property."‡

C. This text does not take effect if there be Sapiṇḍas as far as the fourth. This text is of effect if there be Sapiṇḍas commencing with the fifth. Thus it is explained by

* D. cccclxxv. † D. ccclxxxi. where the last half verse differs entirely.

‡ Do. dxiii.

the commentators. By others *however the arrangement is made (as follows):—If there be six relations such as sister's son etc. of the six persons beginning with the mother's sister, then where a husband succeeds to a childless woman's strîdhana, in case of his default, of the three relations who (are so) through the husband, the husband's younger brother first succeeds to the elder brother's wife's wealth by reason of his greater affinity. In his default the husband's brother's son takes (it). In his default the husband's sister's son takes (it). Where however the mother and father would succeed, then in their default, of the three relations (who are so) through them, the deceased woman's sister's son takes first. In his default her brother's son takes (it). In his default the son-in-law takes it. As by the words "sister's sons etc." we know that the offspring (of sisters is intended), for an affix is there used indicating offspring†, it is proper that males and females (both) should have a claim to the heritage. Others however think that as even on consideration of words (indicating both) males and females in common, we first think of the males, and because we see the explanatory text:—

"Therefore women are powerless and do not get a share"—

that therefore males only and not females succeed to the heritage.

Reunion. Next the heritage of reunited persons is explained. In regard to this Manu (ix., 210 says):—

"If brethren, once divided and living again together as parceners, make a second partition, the shares must in that case be equal; and the first-born shall have no right of deduction." (J.)

C. The meaning is that an extra portion is not to be made for the eldest on partition of reunited (members of a family).

*? J. V. (Dāyabhāga), iv., iii., 37. †Pāṇini, iv., 1. 148.

(Do. 211):—

"Should the eldest or youngest of several brothers be deprived of his share (*by a civil death on his entrance into the fourth order*), or should any one of them die, his (*vested interest in a*) share shall not (wholly) be lost." (J.)

C. Of these males who by the text:—

"Great sinners do not deserve a share"—

whether he be the eldest or the youngest, may die barred from a share by murder of a Brahman or the like (crime), or may go abroad, his share is not lost, nor may those (who) are reunited simply take it. To answer the question—what is to be done then? He says:—

(Do. 212):—

"But (*if he leave neither son, nor wife, nor daughter, nor father, nor mother*) his uterine brothers and sisters, and such brothers as were reunited (after a separation), shall assemble and divide his share equally." (J.)

C. The uterine brothers should come together and divide the share of the degraded man who is dead or has gone abroad, and reunited brothers, though not uterine brothers, should share (it) with uterine brothers not reunited. They take because of the community of origin even in default of community of wealth with (their) uterine brother; or because of the community of wealth even in default of community of origin with their half-brother. So the uterine sisters of the deceased should divide (it) equally with the above mentioned uterine (and also) reunited brothers.

"And the brothers who are reunited."

Ācārya Viçvarūpa says that the mention of "brothers" is in order, on reunion with another (such as) a father or uncle, to include (his) wife etc.

Yājñavalkya (says ii., 138) in regard to this:—

"The share of a reunited brother, the reunited brother should give or take; but that of an uterine brother the uterine brother (should give or take) if (a son) be born or (if his brother) die."

C. Reunited (property) is wealth (that has been) divided (and) again mixed up. He whose this is, (is) a reunited (person).

(Thus) Bṛhaspati has given the rule regarding reunited persons:—

"He who (having been) divided, (is) again established out of affection together with (his) father or brother, or with his uncle even, is said to be reunited."

One who is reunited should give to (a child) born after (the partition) of a wife (widow) whose pregnancy was not detected at the time of partition, the portion of the deceased (person) reunited (with him). Or in default of such a son, (he) the reunited should take the deceased's share; not the wife etc. A reunited uterine brother should give the share of a deceased reunited uterine brother to (his son when) born. To answer the question—how is the succession, if a reunited childless (man) be dead, and there be a half-brother reunited and a uterine brother not reunited? he (Yājñ.) says (ii., 139):—

"A half brother (who is) reunited should not take the wealth of a half brother (who is not reunited); an (uterine brother) should get it though not reunited, not one born of another mother."*

C. "A half brother"—a reunited brother by a fellow wife should not get all the wealth but half. "Though not reunited," he should get the other half. In answer to the question who is the (one) not united? he says—"reunited"—that is to say, a reunited full brother, "not one born of another mother." In this case the explanation is to be made by supplying the word "exclusively"; (one) though reunited, if born of another mother, should not exclusively take the wealth of (one) reunited. If however he be a full brother, though not reunited, he should take it. Here because the

---

*In this verse there is much difference between the MSS. and Stenzler's edition. I follow Varadarāja.

word "though" occurs, a positive prohibition—"certainly not one born of another mother"—would be inferred; therefore (it) is not (here) to be inserted.* As in the case of a reunited (person), wives cease to inherit, they must (therefore) be supported till (their) death. So Nārada (xiii., 26 a.) says with reference to reunited persons:—

"But let the brothers allow a maintenance to his women for life." (Bühler.)

What has been said (regarding) the succession to the property of a reunited (person), some say (applies) in default of sons, wives and daughters. Thus Bṛhaspati (says):—

"When any one dies or goes abroad, anyhow his share is not lost; it is ordained for his uterine brother. But she who is his daughter must get a share out of it. This is the rule for one deceased without leaving children, a wife or father."

But by Nārada's text (xiii., 26):—

"Let the brothers allow a maintenance to his women for life, provided these preserve unsullied the bed of their lord. But if they behave otherwise, the brethren may resume that allowance"— (Bühler.)

is it not inferred that even if there be a wife (the brothers have) the succession? Quite so; if you take the word wife (patnī) in the sense of women who get inheritance, there is no contradiction by Nārada's text.

The learned say that in those Smṛtis in which the words woman (yoshit), widow, female (nārī), woman (strī), spouse (bhāryā) etc. are used, they (intend that they) are to be supported; but in those smṛtis in which wife (patnī) is used, in such, a succession to heritage is declared. In regard to this Bṛhaspati makes a distinction:—

"Whoever among reunited (persons) gains wealth by learning, heroism etc., two shares are to be given him; the rest share equally."†

Kātyāyana (says):—

In default (of nearer heirs) reunited (brothers) are to be considered

*Abridged from Mit. ii., ix., 8—11 †D. ccccix.

heirs of those who are reunited, and separated (brothers) of those separated; (if) childless, they reciprocally share (the estates)."*

C. On the death of any (one) of reunited (brothers) without children, (his) wealth (goes to) one reunited; so also on the death of any (one) not reunited and without children, his wealth (becomes the property) of those not reunited. In their default it belongs to the others. If reunited (persons) die without (leaving) children, (i. e.) without descendents, those who are not reunited take their wealth; so if (persons) not reunited die without (leaving) children, those who are reunited take their wealth.

Yājñavalkya makes a distinction in regard to this (ii., 137):—

"The heirs of a Vānaprastha (hermit), ascetic, (a) Brahmacāri (celibate) are in (the following) order: the ācārya, a good pupil, a brother in religion and a fellow-resident of the same hermitage."

In regard to this Vishṇu (says) (xvii., 15 & 16):—

"Let the spiritual teacher (ācārya) take the wealth of a hermit (Vānaprastha). Or his pupil (may take it)." (Bühler.)

END.

* Do. cccexxvii.

CORRIGENDA.

Page 3,	line 3,	For: without desire	Read: without sensual desire
4	14-16:	Sir W. Jones's translation runs:— "The portion deducted for the eldest is a twentieth part *(of the heritage)*, with the best of all the chattels; for the middlemost, half of that, *(or a fortieth)*; for the youngest, a quarter of it, *(or an eightieth)*."	
5	28	For: of the immovable	Read: of all the immovable
8	19	„ anûbandhya (sacrifice)	„ anûbandhya sacrifice
10	21	„ three shares	„ three parts
„	25	„ unmarried daughters	„ *unmarried* daughters
„	28	„ so they who	„ and they who
12	5	„ *(of his brothers)*	Thus the Mss. Manu has *father*.
„	11	„ (ii., 6, 2, 14 & 15)	Read: (ii., 6, 14, 14 and 15)
13	1	„ profit by heirs	„ profit by him
„	14	„ to a region of punishment.	„ *to a region of punishment.*
„	17	„ that son and	„ *that son and*
15	16, 17	„ visible property gain	„ visible property cleared of gain
„	32	„ (ii., 122)	„ (ii., 120)
16	19	„ from his father	„ from his grandfather
17	20	„ in equality	„ inequality
19	20	„ For Çûdra	„ For a Çûdra
20	14	„ Çûdra	„ Çûdrâ
„	16	„ non	„ nor
„	18	„ be his."	„ be his own."
23	11	„ all his	„ (all) his
„	18	„ has no issue	„ have no issue
„	21	„ had been given	„ has been given
„	32	„ just causes	„ just cause
„	33	„ son.	„ son self-given.
24	3	„ virtue	„ virtues
„	4	„ *adoptor*	„ *adopter*
„	9	„ unfaithful wife	„ *(unfaithful)* wife
25	11	„ legistators	„ legislators
„	34	„ Manu	„ (Manu)
26	1, 2	Sir W. Jones's translation runs:— "And, when the son of the body has taken an account of the paternal inheritance, let him give a sixth part of it to the son of the wife begotten by a kinsman, *(before his father's recovery)*, or a fifth part, *(if that son be eminently* virtuous)."	
30	9, 10	These two lines should be in small type.	

Page	Line	For	Read
Page 31,	line 10,	For: next	Read: next;
„	18	dele (visible)	
32	note ‡	For: pramitasya	„ pramitasya
33	23	„ uterine brothers of the father	„ uterine (brothers) among the brothers of the father
34	14	„ given (her)	„ given by (her)
„	28-39	„ The texts of Apastamba and Manu have apparently been inverted by a copyist.	
39	1	„ Others say	Read: Others (say)
43	15	„ to sons by	„ to two sons by
44	25	„ their property	„ that property
46	22	„ from household furniture	„ for household furniture
47	30	„ such bandhus	„ (such) bandhus
49	3	„ in order"	„ in their order."
„	32	„ take or give	„ take and give back
53	6	„ who by the	„ whoever by the

www.ingramcontent.com/pod-product-compliance
Lightning Source LLC
Chambersburg PA
CBHW021524270326
41930CB00008B/1081
* 9 7 8 3 3 3 7 8 1 7 0 8 4 *